"For a biblical look at a God who puts questioning God at the heart of the religious quest and builds participation into the very design of the universe, see Rob Fringer and Jeff Lane's stimulating and provocative *Theology of Luck*."

—Leonard Sweet
Best-Selling Author, Professor (Drew University,
George Fox University), and Chief Contributor to Sermons.com

"Few books bring together essential questions and then offer a profound and multifaceted theological answer. But this one does so in a powerful and convincing way, as it presents the God of love, relationship, and participation as the answer to life's perplexing questions. A bit of luck may have led you to this book, but I hope you freely read it. And I hope you cooperate with God's efforts to use this book for good!"

—Thomas Jay Oord
Professor of Theology and Philosophy
Northwest Nazarene University

"For those convinced of God's existence but wondering what kind of God they believe in, this book serves as fresh food for thought. Jeff and Rob provide us with some fresh perspective on very ancient questions. Their reflections will stimulate your own mind and heart to wonder all over again."

—Reggie McNeal
Author of *Missional Renaissance* and *Get Off Your Donkey!*

"Throughout the centuries humanity has grappled with its understanding of God. Often God becomes clouded in the context of Christian practices and the secular world. Fringer and Lane challenge us to strip away the trappings we may have inadvertently brought into our relationship with God and find a sense of renewal so that our lives can be reflections of him."

—Carla Sunberg
President, Nazarene Theological Seminary

D1736375

"*Theology of Luck* will rock your world and will move to the front burner the honest conversation all kingdom-minded believers long to have about God, fate, prayer, career, choice, sovereignty, God's part and our part in his redemptive mission, and above all the theology of luck. Thank you, Rob and Jeff, for this gift. May it spawn conversations and actions that change us and change the world."

—Eric Swanson
Leadership Network
Coauthor of *The Externally Focused Church* and *To Transform a City*

"Religions from around the world have attributed luck and fate to the gods. They have tried to manipulate 'the gods' through magic, rituals, and incantations. So, if this tends to be what happens in religion, is Christianity just another conception of fate, luck, and magic? Fringer and Lane challenge this notion head on. For our authors, thinking Christianly is based on different assumptions about God, events in the world, and our responses as people who base our actions on faith in Jesus Christ. I highly recommend this thoughtful yet accessible discussion of our interaction with God in a world filled with uncertainty."

—Ron Benefiel
Dean of the School of Theology and Christian Ministry
Point Loma Nazarene University

THEOLOGY OF LUCK

Theology

of

LUCK

Fate, Chaos, *and* Faith

ROB A. FRINGER *and* JEFF K. LANE

BEACON HILL PRESS
OF KANSAS CITY

Copyright © 2015 by Rob A. Fringer and Jeff K. Lane
Beacon Hill Press of Kansas City
PO Box 419527
Kansas City, MO 64141
www.BeaconHillBooks.com

ISBN 978-0-8341-3496-6

Printed in the
United States of America

Cover Design: Jeff Gifford
Interior Design: Sharon Page

Library of Congress Cataloging-in-Publication Data

Fringer, Rob A.
　Theology of luck : fate, chaos, and faith / Rob A. Fringer and Jeff K. Lane.
　　pages cm
　Includes bibliographical references.
　ISBN 978-0-8341-3496-6 (pbk.)
　1. God (Christianity) 2. Providence and government of God--Christianity. 3. Faith.
4. Fortune—Miscellanea. 5. Free will and determinism. 6. Liberty—Religious aspects—
Christianity. 7. Fate and fatalism—Religious aspects—Christianity. I. Title.
　BT103.F76 2015
　231'.5—dc23

　　　　　　　　　　　　　　　　　　　　　　　　　　2015020102

All Scripture quotations, unless otherwise indicated, are taken from the *Holy Bible, New International Version*® (NIV®). Copyright © 1973, 1978, 1984, 2011 by Biblica, Inc.® Used by permission. All rights reserved worldwide.

Scripture quotations marked KJV are from the King James Version.

Permission to quote from the following copyrighted versions of the Bible is acknowledged with appreciation.

The *New American Standard Bible*® (NASB®), © The Lockman Foundation 1960, 1962, 1963, 1968, 1971, 1972, 1973, 1975, 1977, 1995.

The *New Revised Standard Version* (NRSV) of the Bible, copyright 1989 by the Division of Christian Education of the National Council of the Churches of Christ in the USA. All rights reserved.

The *Message* (MSG). Copyright © 1993. Used by permission of NavPress Publishing Group.

The Internet addresses, email addresses, and phone numbers in this book are accurate at the time of publication. They are provided as a resource. Beacon Hill Press of Kansas City does not endorse them or vouch for their content or permanence.

10 9 8 7 6 5 4 3 2 1

Dedicated to our loving wives:
Vanessa Fringer and Kelley Lane

● ● ●

CONTENTS

· · ·

INTRODUCTION

● ● ●

It is said that what we believe determines how we live. Is this axiom true? Many looking at the church from the outside do not believe this to be the case. They look at the church and see no marked difference between those inside and those outside. Why?

Option No. 1: The axiom is not true, and belief does not truly determine action.

Option No. 2: Those outside the church have an erroneous understanding of what we believe, which has led to unrealistic expectations of how we should live.

Option No. 3: We do not fully believe in this God or in the Word, and something deep within us actually prevents us from fully giving our lives over to God.

Option No. 4: Our lives actually do reflect the God in whom we believe.

There is likely some truth in each of these options as well as other possibilities not listed. However, the concern of this book is with options 3 and 4, which are closely related. The following story will help disclose our point.

In James A. Michener's bestselling novel *The Source*,[1] he tells the story of Urbaal and his second wife, Timna, who live in Makor, a fictitious town in western Galilee, around 2202 BC. During a time of impending war, Timna's firstborn son, at only six months old, is selected along with seven other firstborn sons to be sacrificed to Melak, the god of death and war. Timna is a foreigner to this land and does not necessarily believe in their gods. For this reason, she is devastated by the decision and wants her husband either to rebel against the priests who have made the selection or to flee from Makor to save her son. Urbaal, however, has grown up in these lands and is fully convinced of the various gods' powers. Furthermore, he has already offered three other firstborn sons, who came from his first wife and two of his slave girls.

Though Urbaal has some remorse, his mind is preoccupied by the realization that his willing obedience had bettered his chances to win the yearly Astarte contest. Astarte is the goddess of fertility, and each year one lucky man wins the privilege of making an offering to this goddess by spending a week with a sixteen-year-old virgin who has been selected as the newest temple prostitute. With the pain of her son's death still fresh in her mind, Timna watches as Urbaal is selected the winner and exuberantly claims his prize.

"And while others celebrated she walked away slowly homeward, seeing life in a new and painful clarity: *with different gods her husband Urbaal would have been a different man.*"[2]

This fictional story is both sad and insightful. Timna's conclusion reveals a profound truth—namely, that the gods we believe in and serve often define our reality. While this truth will resonate with many readers, other minds will quickly move toward thoughts of other religions and other gods.

But what about our God? Who is the God we serve? What do Scripture, tradition, reason, and experience actually reveal about this God, and is it consistent with what we believe, what we have been taught, and what we have taught others?

For far too long, Christians have accepted pictures of God that are not only scripturally fictitious but also harmful to our world. The results have been twofold: Either the inconsistencies and unfathomability of our particular picture of God have prevented us from fully embracing God (option 3), or we have fully embraced a false picture of God and, therefore, had our lives conformed to that image (option 4). The former has led to a lukewarm and complacent church that has seen many walk away unsatisfied. The latter has led to horrific acts of war, injustice, and hate, such as the Crusades, the Holocaust, and—more recently—the Westboro Baptist Church in Topeka, Kansas.

Stanley Hauerwas and William Willimon are correct that the church has been preoccupied with apologetics, trying to prove the existence of God in an attempt to combat atheism. However, "Christian theology should be preoccupied with the more biblical question, What *kind* of God exists?"[3]

Inconsistent and unhealthy pictures of God have led to inconsistent and unhealthy followers. With a different God, we would be different people. We therefore seek to deconstruct false pictures of God and reveal a healthier, more consistent, and more scriptural picture of God. Before we can convince the world that this God exists, we must first evidence a God worthy of belief, a God who can actually transform lives and the world.

For this reason, our book begins with the assumption that the God introduced in the Old Testament and made known through Christ in the New Testament does, in fact, exist. Admittedly, our primary audience consists of those who already believe in the existence of this God and who probably already have some type of connection to this God.

However, we hope that all who read this book, whether or not they believe God exists, will consider the feasibility of the God we describe and the impact that belief in this God could have on our world. It is our humble conviction that this particular God is in fact the hope of the world and that as Christians start to grapple with the nature and character of this God, and begin to wholeheartedly embrace this God, they will give their lives over to this God and to God's mission in this world.

The second focus of the book is to discuss our response and responsibility to this God and this world. It is our hope that as we unfold this particular picture of God, readers will fall deeply in love with God, either for the first time or all over again. We believe an embrace of this God will instill within each person a deep desire for commitment to the mission of God in this world. We hope this book will move you to deeper relationship and deeper community.

The book is divided into three sections, each suggesting a movement away from a particular understanding and toward another and each seeking to answer two specific questions related to God and humanity.

Section 1 (chapters 1, 2, and 3) explores the movement from *fate* to *faith*, seeking to answer these questions: What kind of God is this? and What kind of system did this God create?

Section 2 (chapters 4, 5, and 6) explores the movement from *magic* to *mystery*, seeking to answer these questions: How is God active in the world? and What is our place in this world?

Section 3 (chapters 7, 8, and 9) explores the movement from *destiny* to *desire*, seeking to answer these questions: What is our response to this God? and What is our responsibility in this world?

SECTION 1
THE MOVEMENT FROM FATE TO FAITH

○ ○ ○

What kind of God is this?

What kind of system did this God create?

1
FREEING GOD

● ● ●

Written by God?

"Did God break my neck?"

Joshua Prager[1] has struggled with this question for more than half his life. It is the question that has made him stop believing in God. On May 16, 1990, Joshua and his companions were traversing a winding hill in Jerusalem when a runaway truck carrying four tons of ceramic tiles hit them. One person was killed, many sustained serious injuries, and Joshua was paralyzed from the neck down.

Plagued by questions of *why*, Joshua set out twenty-two years after the crash to find the man who had been driving the runaway truck, seeking answers and some semblance of closure. Yet Joshua's encounter with Abed, the driver of the runaway truck, left him well short of settled. Instead of showing remorse, Abed spent most of their conversation complaining about his own suffering, taking no responsibility for his part in the tragedy. But the most difficult part for Joshua was Abed's suggestion that everything that happened that day was *maktoob* (the Arabic term for "letter," or "written," which communicates the idea that events are fated to occur for divine purposes). Abed described how he had lived an unholy life before the crash and how God had ordained this wreck to transform his journey. From where Abed sat, Joshua and all of the victims in the crash were part of a grand scheme that had been written by God to get Abed's attention.

Overcome by a multitude of emotions, Joshua had to come to terms with the possibility that God might have caused these events. As difficult as this idea was, it actually provided him with some momentary relief. After all, if God had his hands in every activity, then there was likely some purpose behind it all, and at least Joshua had some answers.

Yet it was hard for Joshua to say thank you to this kind of God, especially in his current situation. The words of this reckless truck driver continued to haunt him. How could it be said it was God's will? Eventually Joshua abandoned that belief. As he began to reflect and research, he realized that what others saw as divine orchestration could simply be a perfect storm of potentialities. Today, when he is asked about the cause of the accident, he describes how his neck snapped because of the lack of a proper headrest in his seat. He speaks about how the driver of the runaway truck had twenty-six driving violations, how the road they traveled was notorious for tragic accidents, with more than 144 reported and many casualties, and how bad the weather conditions were that day.

Joshua's story may sound outlandish, but it is just one of many similar episodes. The times, places, and events are different, but the basic stories are the same. People faced with disease, death, or loss cry out for answers, and the best this world can give them is either purposeless chance or divine, random purpose.

God must have had a reason for the death of that child.

God must be trying to tell you something through the loss of that job.

That tragedy was meant as a judgment by God.

God is in control; everything happens for a reason.

These types of phrases and our reactions to them say a lot about our understanding of God. (Or is it a misunderstanding?) Do we really believe God causes events like these as part of some divine plan? Do we really believe our lives, the good and the bad, are already written by God?

A Tale of Two Gods

We are not the first people to ask these questions. Throughout history, people have struggled to understand what God is like and how God intervenes in our world. From Augustine to Calvin, Luther to Barth, great Christian thinkers have tried to give us pictures of who God is and how we can describe and interpret divine activity in the world. Theologians have wrestled with many questions about what God predestines, determines, and allows in our present reality.

One of the great points of interest for theologians is the relationship between God's goodness, God's sovereignty, and the recurrence of evil in the world. The question of whether God causes tragedies such as earthquakes, diseases, or even broken necks for some divine purpose is traditionally called *theodicy*. This term was coined by Gottfried Leibniz, a seventeenth-century philosopher and mathematician, in an essay where he sought to articulate the relationship between the freedom of man and the justice of God.[2] The word itself is a combination of the Greek words for "God" and "justice" and expresses the often presumed tension that exists between the two terms. Just as the persons involved in Joshua Prager's bus accident, Leibniz struggled with whether events were written by God. He wrestled with the relationship between God's power and character and the seeming lack of justice in the world.

Leibniz believed theodicy could be explained by exploring three particular beliefs about God in the world: God's power, God's goodness, and the presence of evil. Leibniz attempted to provide a landscape for how these three realities exist. He postulated that nothing happens without the permission of the universally almighty God, whose every action is consistent with "goodness, justice and holiness."[3] Thus, though our reasoning fails to understand the permitting of evil, that does not dismiss the reality that the world must be as God intended, and because God is good and all-powerful, the present reality must also be "the best of all possible worlds."[4]

Leibniz's views help articulate a popular view of God, one on which people often call when trying to come to grips with the presence of suffering in the world. This first image is what we'll call the *God of control*. Envisioning God as a God of control helps express the powerful nature of God. This God is the one the psalmist speaks about as the Lord who "reigns," who makes the "mountains melt like wax" and "guards the lives of his faithful ones and delivers them from the hand of the wicked" (Ps. 97:1, 5, 10). This God has the whole world in his hands. This is not a God to be taken lightly, because there is no doubt that this God is in charge.

Every image we use to try to express our vision of God has a measure of payoff to it. If there were no benefit to thinking about God in a particular way, then we would abandon that vision for another, more helpful or rewarding one. The positive outcome of these differing views of God is what we'll call *gospels*. The gospel—or good news—of the God of control is that God has a plan, and if we are connected to God, we can rest assured that God will take care of us. In this case, the God of control offers a *gospel of acquiescence*. This God of control is often spoken of in terms of having events predetermined or predestined. This gospel of acquiescence grants a measure of predictability about the world and a comforting simplicity that everything happens for a reason—namely, whatever purpose this God of control has determined should be.

However, though there may be a sense of comfort from the certainty that comes from envisioning this God of control, there is also the potential that this vision creates a level of apathy and complacency among its followers. If we buy into the vision of the God of control, we probably have a theology that settles for a sense of inevitability that this God is at work; therefore, we don't have to be. This is what we'll refer to as a *theology of certainty*. We are willing to trade in some freedom for the comfort that someone greater than us has everything under control, and there is certainly a level of relief that comes from this vision. But is it the best? What kind of life comes from having such a vision of God?

The theology of certainty is present in many of the historical voices of the Christian faith discussing God's control over events of the past and God's influence over the events of the future. From Augustine to Calvin, we see the benefit of understanding the sovereignty of God. We do not suggest that the God of control has no validity in the Christian tradition. In fact, this God seems pretty close to the God we see in the work of Leibniz.

However, Leibniz tries to hold so tightly to the affirmations that God is all powerful and all good that, in a sense, he fails to take seriously the reality of evil. Instead, he seems to dismiss evil as simply part of the plan of this God of control. This flippant dismissal makes him the subject of great critique by the contemporary voices of his day. Voltaire (1694–1778), a renowned historian, philosopher, and prolific writer, was one of these critics and wrote the well-known satire *Candide*[5] in reaction to Leibniz's deterministic God.

The story revolves around a hero named Candide, who is incredibly naïve about the world and its potential dangers. He is greatly influenced by a sage named Pangloss, whose mantra ("things cannot be otherwise than as they are; for as all things have been created for some end, they must necessarily be created for the best end")[6] is a mockery of Leibniz's famous phrase. Through his narrative, Voltaire seeks to disqualify any divine justification for the suffering of humanity by challenging Leibniz's contention that suffering should be accepted as full of meaning and purpose because it comes from the hands of an all-powerful and all-benevolent Creator.

Like many other philosophers of his day, Voltaire was a deist. He was a proponent of God's existence because of the orderly system of the universe, the necessity of a first cause in creation, and the necessity for judgment of good and evil in the end; but he viewed this God as no longer actively participating in the world. For Voltaire, things were not written and were certainly not in their best possible state. Voltaire represents for us the *God of passivity*.

The God of passivity is a completely different vision than the God of control. The God of passivity is still a powerful God but one who has made the choice, in God's vast wisdom, to keep a good distance and let things play out. This is the God who allows death, suffering, and tragedy to occur, not because there is purpose, but simply because that is how the world has been made. This is what we refer to as a *theology of absence*. Theology of absence does not suggest that God is incapable of intervening; simply that God chooses not to intervene. This passive vision of God is best understood as the God who chooses not to show up, and remains silent in the presence of tragedy.

Something positive about the God of passivity is that humanity is allowed to live as it desires. In fact, a theology of absence places a high value on human authority because a theology of absence assumes that no one is coming to the rescue, so we will need to take care of things ourselves. Therefore, the good news from the God of passivity and the theology of absence is the *gospel of autonomy*.

The gospel of autonomy can provide an invigorating sense of pride at the potential of human capability to effect change and progress in the world. It can free us from the burden of inevitability, the doom that things are already written, the weight that robs us of the power to choose our way in the world. This passive vision of God sees the benefit of giving up certainty for the potential of freedom.

However, though many of us may see the gospel of autonomy as a potentially admirable vision for the world, we must also consider the downside. There is no guarantee that this absent God has a plan in place when we want delivery. So, when we cry out with the psalmist, "My God, my God, why have you forsaken me? Why are you so far from saving me, so far from my cries of anguish? My God, I cry out by day, but you do not answer, by night, but I find no rest" (Ps. 22:1-2), we cannot live in the certainty that the God of passivity will come to the rescue. We must also recognize that having a vision of God as absent can often lead to an inflated sense of arrogance in human progress, leaving us vulnerable to our own potential for moral misgivings.

Are the God of control and the God of passivity the only options? Or is it possible to find a third way to understand and respond to the power of God and the presence of evil in our world? Is it possible God needs to be freed from having to fit nicely into either of these two categories?

Setting God Free

The idea of God needing to be set free is, in itself, a little amusing. Nevertheless, these two visions of God are too small, too simplistic, too black and white. Does God either have to be controlling or passive? Could it be that God is more dynamic than that, more relational, more personal, and more complex?

Many of us subscribe to one of the other two models because they are safe. They present a God we can define and, thus, a God we can manipulate or ignore. These are not the picture of God we see in Scripture, however.

A third view presents itself in a *God of relationship*, who partners with creation, working in and through us to bring about beauty in the midst of tragedy. While this idea is not new, the relational nature of God is often ignored, downplayed, or given lip service without application. Why?

Maybe we are scared to talk about God in relational ways because we feel this makes God too much like us. And if God is like us, then how can God save us? We equate *relational* with *human* and *human* with *weakness, vulnerability,* and *fallenness.* Yet we cannot define relational from our perspective. God is the one who first existed in relationship (Father, Son, and Holy Spirit) and who first created relationship (humanity); therefore, God must be the basis for our definition of what true relationship means and what it looks like.

Arguably, the clearest picture we have of the very essence of God, one that exemplifies God's relational nature, is found in the incarnate Christ, the God who became flesh (John 1:14). The Christological hymn of Philippians 2:6-8 provides us with a panoramic view of God in a microscopic look.

[Christ,] Who, being in very nature God,
      did not consider equality with God something to be
        used to his own advantage;
rather, he made himself nothing
      by taking the very nature of a servant,
      being made in human likeness.

And being found in appearance as a man,

  he humbled himself

  by becoming obedient to death—

    even death on a cross!

We look at this passage and are awestruck by the sure absurdity and profundity of it. It presents us with a picture of the self-emptying God who humbled himself to the point of taking on flesh and being a servant, and giving himself on the cross. Here we do not see a dominant and controlling God; neither do we see a passive and distant God. Here we see a God who suffers right alongside creation.

But why would Christ give up everything he had to come and die for sinful humanity? Many who have a view of God as either controlling or passive will wonder why God would act so ungodlike. Herein we miss the main point that a relational view of God can teach us about God's nature. It is not that Christ acted ungodlike, or even abnormal. Rather, Philippians 2:6-8 reveals the very character of the relational God.

Michael Gorman captures this reality in his interpretive paraphrase:

> Although Messiah Jesus was in the form of God, a status people assume means the exercise of power, he acted *in* character—in a shockingly ungodlike manner according to normal but misguided human perceptions of divinity, contrary to what we would expect but, in fact, in accord with true divinity—when he emptied and humbled himself.[7]

Christ's very nature is service and sacrifice because Christ's very nature is love and relationship. Moreover, the incarnation and the cross are proof of these realities. It is not the exaltation of Philippians 2:9-11 that prove Jesus is God but rather the incarnation and the cross.

> Jesus' exaltation is not the divine reward for his incarnation and death as God's suffering servant (as this text is normally interpreted), but divine recognition that his suffering-servant behavior is in fact truly "lordly," even godly, behavior.[8]

What about Yahweh, the God of the Old Testament? Does he also share in the loving, serving nature that defines Christ? Or is Richard Dawkins correct in his caricature:

> The God of the Old Testament is arguably the most unpleasant character in all fiction: jealous and proud of it; a petty, unjust, unforgiving control-freak; a vindictive, bloodthirsty ethnic cleanser; a misogynistic, homophobic, racist, infanticidal, genocidal, filicidal, pestilential, megalomaniacal, sadomasochistic, capriciously malevolent bully.[9]

Dawkins is not alone in his critique of the Old Testament God, nor does the criticism come from atheists and agnostics alone. Very early in the church's history, a bishop named Marcion (ca. AD 85–ca. AD 160) wrote a small work called *Antithesis* that outlined the differences he saw between the Old Testament deity and the New Testament God.

> This god (Yahweh) is the author of evil—there must be another God, after the analogy of the good tree producing its good fruit. In Christ is found a different disposition, one of a simple and pure benevolence—which differs from the Creator. In Christ a new God is revealed. The Creator God is judicial, harsh, and mighty in war. The Supreme God is gentle and simply good and excellent.[10]

Likewise, many Christians today hold similar views, even if they do not verbalize them. It is evident in their lack of attention to the Old Testament, or at least to parts of the Bible that are difficult to swallow.

But is this antithesis warranted? After all, we do not believe in two Gods or even three Gods but, rather, in one God, *tres personae, una substantia*[11] (three persons, one substance). We believe in the Trinity of Father, Son, and Holy Spirit, who together form a perfect community and define relationship; who together are involved in creation, redemption, and sanctification; who together are holy, righteous, magnificent, just, eternal, faithful, forgiving, merciful, sovereign, wise, infinite, self-sufficient, unchanging, and sacrificial; and who together define and encapsulate love!

Therefore, we cannot speak of the character and nature of Christ in the incarnation and cross as displayed in Philippians 2:6-8 as antithetical to that of the Father. Rather, Christ reveals to us the Father (John 1:18; 14:6-11). He reveals the heart of the Godhead, who from Genesis to Revelation pursues his creation, desiring a love relationship and inviting his creatures to embody his love to the world (see, for example, Gen. 1:26-28; Deut. 7:9; Ps. 23:6; Jer. 29:11-13; Zeph. 3:17; John 3:16; Rom. 8:37-39; Eph. 2:4-5; 1 John 4:9-10; Rev. 21:2-5). Surely, we can agree that this God is not the passive god of Voltaire. This God is too active, too involved, to be described as absent or indifferent. What about the controlling god of Leibniz? Does our description of God as relational disprove that God is deterministic, controlling all things—even evil?

Let us return to the incarnation from a different angle. While few would disagree that the incarnation of Christ was part of God's master plan, how do we explain the collateral damage that came along with it? In looking at the larger story of Jesus's birth in Matthew 2:16-18, we read about how God warns Joseph to flee to Egypt to escape the tyrant Herod, who fears this new child will threaten his throne; he therefore orders his legions to kill infants and toddlers, in hopes that Jesus will be one of the casualties.

Is this part of God's master plan? Has God determined in advance for the magi to encounter Herod? Does Herod have a choice in his cruel actions? Has God ordained the death of these infants? Is this just part of the providence of God? Is this just the cost of our salvation and the cost of relationship with this God?

It is important to recognize that events like these are much more complicated than a simple yes or no in relation to God's activity. It is never as simple as hard determinism or passive deism. Frank Tupper, writing on this passage, suggests that "the entanglement of the purpose of God with givens which thwart that purpose remains inevitable. God's good work seldom does not awaken new possibilities of evil."[12] The God who is present in the protection of Jesus and the death of infants is the God who acts, "but God is not the sole shaper of events in human history. God does not control everything, and God does not control anything completely."[13] So, then, the God of the universe is the God who has demonstrated a willingness to initiate but a hesitance to dominate.

This is a difficult concept for many.

What kind of God is this? What kind of God initiates actions that awaken possibilities of evil?

A good God!

What kind of God does not seek to control everything?

A servant God!

What kind of God refuses to dominate and instead gives in to the domination of a cross?

A suffering God!

What kind of God creates with purpose but also with possibilities?

A loving God!

A relational God!

Free Will and Free Grace

Relationship requires freedom—freedom to love and freedom to be indifferent, freedom to accept and freedom to reject. This is the dynamism of the God we serve. The God we serve is not a God of passivity or a God of control. The God we serve creates humanity for relationship then frees us to choose. At least this was the story before the fall.

Prior to the fall, humanity (Adam and Eve) roam in the garden with God, free to do anything they want, even free to disobey (Gen. 2:16-17; 3:6). But this disobedience has consequences that have been made known prior to the act. Disobedience ultimately leads to death, but before that, it leads to a loss of free will. Prior to the fall, humanity is free to sin or free not to sin. As a result of the fall, humanity is no longer free not to sin. Yet this sin does not define us![14]

This foreign object we call *sin* infected and enslaved us (Rom. 5–6). But this is not the end of the story. God did not abandon us after the fall; God reached out to us, through Christ, with grace—a grace that allowed us to be free once again.

John Wesley (1703-91), the father of Methodism, captures this reality when he writes:

> And although I have not an absolute power over my own mind, because of the corruption of my nature, yet through the grace of God assisting me I have a power to choose and do good as well as evil.[15]

Wesley termed this grace *prevenient*, the grace that goes before. Thus we understand that while we are no longer under free will, we are still under free grace. That is, through Christ, our freedom is now due to God's prevenient grace, not human ability—and so it is best to call this freedom free grace.[16] Thus God still allows us the freedom to choose God or reject God—because God desires authentic relationship with us.

Still, our freedom does not come without ramifications for God. For us to be truly free, God must intentionally limit himself. God must limit his actions so as not to control or manipulate humanity. Paradoxically, though, God must also intervene in order to bring about salvation and restoration. As aforementioned, God's intervention, as good as it is, "awakens new possibilities for evil."[17]

We have come full circle to the problem of evil. Evil is the inevitable reality of free will. If humanity is given a choice, it will at points choose wrongly (sometimes intentionally, other times unintentionally). This wrong choice—that which is contrary to the heart of God—is sin, and it leads to broken relationships and broken people and death. God could have taken free will away and made us all robots who always make the right decisions. God could have created us with free will, then abandoned us.

Instead, this relational God, who desires nothing more and nothing less than authentic, intimate relationship with creation, gave us free will. Then, when we messed up, God offered us free grace through the death and resurrection of Jesus Christ. Now, if we choose to disobey, God will still pursue us with unassailable devotion and love—yet never control.

Evil is certainly a problem, and it does not make sense. It, like love, is a mystery. Our questions abound about this world, and our place in it, and the puzzling and hurtful actions of others (as well as our own hurtful actions); and one day we may have all the answers, but for now, we must wrestle with this loving, dynamic God who is ever present through the pains and the joys.

A God Who's Willing to Wrestle

At its core, love is expansive, which means it must reach out, must create, must envelop. Herein lies the answer to the question you have all been thinking as you read through this chapter: *Why did God do it?* If what we have claimed is true:

1. If God created us with free will and now continues to give us free grace;

2. If God knew we would inevitably disobey and that this would unleash all hell;

3. If God knew that in creating us he must limit himself;

4. If God knew that he would also have to suffer . . .

. . . then *why?* Why create humanity?

LOVE.

Love is the only answer. Because God *is* love (1 John 4:16), and love is ever-expanding. Love seeks out relationship, and where there is none, love creates the potential for it. However, love does not force itself, because that would not be love. The greatest attribute of love is not what it does or does not do, not what it says or does not say, but, rather, that it is present.

Interestingly enough, this is the most dominant picture of God throughout Scripture: God is the God who is present—in the midst of celebration and in the midst of suffering. In fact, this is the essence of God's holy name. The Hebrew name *Yahweh* derives from the Hebrew verb meaning "to be." God is the great "I AM" (Exod. 3:14), which is another way of saying that God is a present God.

When you look at God's interactions with his people, you see that God continually tries to place himself in the middle of them. Whether it be the ark of the covenant or the tabernacle; the temple or the commandments; the judges, priests, kings, or prophets; or Jesus himself, God continues to insert himself in our midst in an attempt to reveal God's love for us and God's desire for genuine relationship, at great cost to himself.

God does not desire relationship because God is self-consumed, and it's certainly not because God is needy. God does not seek to force himself upon us or coerce us; God is not trying to guilt or shame us. But God is trying to persuade us. God is trying to reveal the extent of his love to us and, in so doing, draw us to himself. In fact, as we shall see, this God does not mind wrestling with creation and does not mind when creation wrestles back, as long as it is motivated by love and the desire for genuine relationship.

True love is always messy. It is not the fairy tale we read about in made-up stories. It is a give-and-take, up-and-down, struggling-for-understanding kind of love that is genuine and painful at points but full of joy and hope and peace. This is what God invites us to.

The God we have been speaking about is the God who offers us the *gospel of participation*. Not only does this God love us enough to die for us, but this God also loves us enough to involve us in God's redemptive plan for the world. This loving partnership does not guarantee that life will not be messy, but it also reminds us that this God has proven he will never leave us alone.

This space to work together calls us to take on the responsibility of being God's people in the world. This vision of wrestling with God leaves room in our philosophy for a *theology of luck*. The presence of that luck is what reminds us that we serve neither the God of control nor the God of passivity but, instead, a God of relationship who serves, sacrifices, and remains present. The good news of this relational God is that he calls us to real participation with him to bring about the world as he desires. This vision of God is what we invite you to explore with us.

Questions for Further Reflection or Small Group Discussion

1. What tragic experiences have you had in your own life? How have these experiences shaped your view of God?

2. How do you think you would have responded if you were Joshua Prager, and Abed told you that your injury had a divine purpose?

3. Have you ever heard of the term *theodicy*? How was it defined for you?

4. If you had to choose between Leibniz's view of God and Voltaire's, whose would you choose? Why?

5. Reread the two versions of Philippians 2:6-8 that we have provided (the NIV version as well as the Gorman paraphrase). What differences do you notice? Which one resonates with you more deeply?

6. What was your first reaction when you read the description of God from Richard Dawkins? Have you ever thought of God in those terms?

7. Do you believe that relationship requires freedom— even the freedom to reject God?

8. Do you like the idea of being in a relationship with a God who wrestles with us? Why or why not?

For Further Study

Beginner to Intermediate

Boyd, Gregory A. *Is God to Blame? Beyond Pat Answers to the Problem of Suffering*. Downers Grove, IL: InterVarsity Press, 2003.

Oord, Thomas Jay. *Science of Love: The Wisdom of Well-Being*. Philadelphia: Templeton Foundation Press, 2004.

Taylor, Richard S. *What Every Christian Ought to Know: Basic Answers to Questions of the Faith*. Kansas City: Beacon Hill Press of Kansas City, 2002.

More Advanced

Boyd, Gregory A. *Satan and the Problem of Evil: Constructing a Trinitarian Warfare Theodicy.* Downers Grove, IL: InterVarsity Press, 2001.

Gorman, Michael. *Inhabiting the Cruciform God: Kenosis, Justification, and Theosis in Paul's Narrative Soteriology.* Grand Rapids: Eerdmans, 2009.

Morgan, Christopher W., and Robert A. Peterson, eds. *Suffering and the Goodness of God.* Wheaton, IL: Crossway Books, 2008.

2
LUCKY?

• • •

Unintended Consequences

When we wrote this chapter, one of the world's most powerful typhoons on record, Haiyan (known as Yolanda by the locals), had just devastated the Philippines. No doubt, many of you remember some of the pictures that followed that storm and some of the stories of loss, pain, and destruction. One story that caught our attention was called "There Is Indeed a God" and was written by a Filipino reporter named Erwin Tulfo.[1] It was an autobiographical account of his near-death encounter while trying to report on the storm. He recounted how he and his team had been trapped by falling trees and raging floodwaters, and then he wrote:

> Since we had nowhere else to run and it appeared that we would either drown or be blown away by Yolanda's powerful winds, I prayed to Jesus with these simple words, "Cover us Lord with your most precious blood that you have shed, and protect us with the painful wounds inflicted upon you."[2]

In what can be described as a miraculous turn of events, Tulfo and his team survived, and he credited God with saving him and reaffirming his faith. He concluded the article with these words:

> I realized one thing. If it is your time to go, you can't stop it. However, if you ask him to put it on hold, he may just do that provided that it will be for your good and that of your loved ones and above all, for his greater glory. After all, he owns our lives.[3]

So, did God really save Erwin Tulfo and his crew?

Our first instinct is to say yes. We want to believe God is able to do this and much more. We want to hear stories that restore our hope in God's love and power. We want to believe it is true because we want to believe it would happen to us if we were in a similar situation one day.

Yet there is a huge, albeit unintended, consequence of Tulfo's story and others like it. There were 6,340 confirmed fatalities from Typhoon Yolanda, and an additional 1,061 missing/presumed dead. Was Tulfo the only one of these more than 7,000 people who cried out to Jesus for rescue? Assuming he was not, did God ignore the other cries? If so, why? Furthermore, Erwin admits that before this event he was not a devout follower of Christ. Of the 7,000-plus people who died or are presumed dead, some of them had to have been Christians.[4] Does God save unbelievers before believers?

No doubt there are many already coming to God's rescue, trying to justify why God saved Erwin and not others:

God knew Erwin was close to believing, and that is why he saved him.

God saved Erwin for a purpose because he was a well-known reporter and could provide an amazing testimony to a larger audience.

What about all the people who didn't die whose stories we don't know? Why do we focus on the ones who died rather than the great number of people God did save?

God can do whatever he wants; who are we to question his ways?

While all these statements are hypothetically possible, they form a picture of God that the world would not be very comfortable with, and neither should Christians. Why does it matter to us what the world thinks of our God? Because it matters to God. God loves all people and desires for them to know who God is. God is not the fickle, angry, arrogant, and indifferent God Christians have often portrayed, the one who loves whom he wants and hates whom he wants, the one who randomly chooses to save some while watching others be crushed and drowned. Rather, the God of relationship, presence, and love we see in Scripture is a God who wants to save people and who wants people to know who he really is.

This same God is the God who enters into covenant with Abram for the purpose of blessing all peoples through him (Gen. 12:3). The God who sends Jonah to Nineveh to reveal himself so the citizens of Nineveh might repent and enter into relationship with God (Jon. 4:11). The God who delivers Israel from captivity so the nations might know who God really is and that he is the God who keeps his promise (Ezek. 36:16-38). The humble servant God who comes and defeats sin and death on a cross to provide a way of salvation to the whole world (John 3:16-17). This is the God we need to reveal to the world!

Complex

The world is much more complex than we often understand it to be, and we need a theology that embraces that complexity. Easy answers and clichés about God do not help anyone. In the end, the only thing they do is provide some people with a false self-worth and false comfort, and others with a picture of God they want nothing to do with.

So how do we explain seemingly miraculous events such as those described in Erwin's account? How do we explain devastating events such as the more than 7,000 people who did not survive or the additional tens of thousands of people who were injured, as well as the hundreds of thousands of those displaced? If God is not to be given credit for the rescue and not to be blamed for the deaths, then what other options are there?

Is it possible that Erwin was lucky and the others were not? Is this idea really the indictment against God that we think it is?

Let us start by defining what we mean by *luck*. Luck is the unintended consequences (both positive and negative) of events without a divine causer, and where there is a human causer, it lacks reason.[5] We could use similar words like *chance*, *coincidence*, *fortune*, *accident*, and so on. However, luck seems to encompass most of these and is a familiar concept to most people, both inside and outside the church, while not having a clear, uniform definition. Furthermore, the idea of luck has both positive and negative connotations.

We want to stress the "without a divine causer" part of our definition. For those who have always viewed God as fully controlling everything, this will be a hard pill to swallow. Nevertheless, in a relational system such as the one God has created, luck is a natural part, and this does not negate God's authority. As John Sanders writes:

> Genuine accidents or unintended events, both good and bad, do happen, for that is the sort of world God establishes. Does this mean that the world is out of God's control? Again, it depends on what is meant by control. God is not in control in the sense that absolutely nothing happens that God does not specifically want to happen. After all, God is fundamentally opposed to sin, yet there is sin. God is in control in the sense that he shoulders the responsibility for creating this type of world.[6]

If we believe God created human beings for genuine relationship, then God had to give them the choice (free will/free grace) to willingly enter into this relationship.

If God gave us a choice, then he had to limit his control, while still being ever present.

If this choice and freedom are real, then there must be real consequences to our actions—some good, some bad, some neutral.

If God has given this same freedom to everyone, then inevitably, people's choices will affect other people—sometimes positively, sometimes negatively, sometimes neutrally. This means that one person's choice can actually take another person's choice away or cause it to have an unintended consequence.

It therefore seems likely that the cause of many events will not be God but some other person(s) and that some people, in relation to those around them, may find themselves in the wrong place at the wrong time or in the right place at the right time. The former we tend to call bad luck and the latter, good luck.

Notice what we are *not* saying. We are not saying everything is a matter of luck. We are not saying God does not cause some things. We are only saying that many things can only be explained by luck, good or bad.

So, for instance, Michael makes the choice to get drunk, hop in his car, and try to drive home. His series of choices has actually infringed upon every other person whom Michael meets for the rest of the night. Janice makes the choice to run across the street to the local market to buy some milk and steps off the sidewalk just as Michael erratically and speedily turns the corner. The two collide, and Janice is immediately killed.

God did not cause this event to take place, nor did God stop the event from taking place. Michael made bad decisions, and Janice was in the wrong place at the wrong time; bad choices for Michael, bad luck for Janice. But the story doesn't end there.

Sonya is in the hospital on life support waiting for a heart transplant, and Janice's heart is still in good condition. Furthermore, Sonya is next on the waiting list to receive a heart, she is a perfect match with Janice, and she is close enough for the medical professionals to get the heart to her on time. Coincidence?

From Sonya's family's perspective, this heart is a godsend. In fact, they and their friends have been praying for this miracle. So have their prayers been answered? Did their prayers cost Janice her life? Did God cause Michael to drive drunk, and Janice to cross the road, just so Sonya could get a heart? Or was Sonya just in the right place at the right time? Bad luck for Janice, good luck for Sonya.

As we can see, it is always more complex when we look at the larger picture and when we take other people and their situations into consideration.

What about natural disasters?

This is indeed a difficult question, since such events are not brought about by human action or inaction. Who is to blame for this? Christopher Wright, in his book *The God I Don't Understand: Reflections on Tough Questions of Faith*,[7] does a great job outlining the two most basic answers to this question and their shortcomings.

The first view is that natural disasters are a result of God's cursing of the ground after the fall (Gen. 3:17-19).[8] From this perspective, God is indirectly responsible, and humanity (or at least, Adam and Eve) is directly responsible. The problem with this view is that "only some unfortunate people suffer the effects in our fallen world because they happen to live in the 'wrong' place, but all of us collectively as a human race bear the blame."[9] This does not seem fair, logical, or gracious. In other words, this does not sound like the work of God.

The second view sees natural disasters as part of the judgment of God. Thus, God is directly the cause of these events, but they are usually brought about by humanity's moral failures. There can be no doubt that Scripture speaks of God's judgment extensively and that it even speaks about some natural disasters as related to God's judgment (e.g., Gen. 6:5-7; Exod. 7–12). Yet these cases are rare, and when they do appear, they are plainly stated. Furthermore, Jesus clearly speaks against this logic at other points (e.g., Luke 13:1-5; John 9:1-3).

Thus, we can deduce that the situations where the connection is made are the exception rather than the rule. A major problem with this view, like the last one, is that those who suffer God's so-called judgment are amassed in specific locations where natural disasters occur frequently. Thus, God's judgment seems arbitrary and comes with lots of collateral damage.

There is no good explanation for natural disasters! Whatever the cause of these kinds of events, we can agree they are part of the brokenness of this world; a world God is moving toward restoration (Isa. 65, 66; Rev. 21).

But for those who find themselves caught in the chaos of these horrors, we must conclude that the majority of the time, it is just a matter of bad luck. It is not a matter of fair or unfair, right or wrong, good or bad. These are out of our control. But what is in our control is the way we respond to these events and to the people who remain standing, those trying to make sense of the devastation and find ways to move forward. *Bad luck* may not be the best possible answer to give these people, but it is far better than "God had a reason." It is probably best if our response is the same as God's—silent but present, mourning with them, listening as they cry out in anger and anguish, and helping them move forward when they are ready.

Fate, Free Will, and Luck

If some things are out of our control, then do we really have free will/free grace? This paradox is complex, and the answer is yes and no. Morally and spiritually, we still have the freedom to choose or not choose God and to choose either what we will do in a particular situation or how we will react to a particular situation. Yet the irony of God's relational creation is that everything is intrinsically interrelated.

Thus, my choices affect you, and vice versa. Likewise, our decisions affect the earth itself, which in turn will affect other humans. Also, the brokenness of this world post-fall means that there will always be uncontrollable forces thrust upon us. Furthermore, there is the reality that God is still active in the world and that, at points along the time line, God *will* intervene in order to help bring about God's master plan of redemption and restoration of creation. When we combine all these factors, we find the irony that free will/free grace within a relational system often impedes choice while simultaneously not being divinely preordained.

This paradox is the place of luck or chance.

The complexities of these phenomena make it difficult to understand and difficult to articulate and have profound impact on how we understand God, our world, and ourselves. Moreover, the complexities lead to widely differing opinions, which is not a recent development. The first-century Jewish historian Flavius Josephus, articulating the differences in belief among the various Jewish sects, wrote:

> Now for the Pharisees, they say that some actions, but not all, are the work of fate, and some of them are in our own power, and that they are liable to fate, but are not caused by fate. But the sect of the Essenes affirm, that fate governs all things, and that nothing befalls men but what is according to its determination. And for the Sadducees, they

take away fate, and say there is no such thing, and that the events of human affairs are not at its disposal; but they suppose that all our actions are in our own power, so that we are ourselves the cause of what is good, and receive what is evil from our own folly.[10]

The Essenes and Sadducees are at opposite spectrums, with the former holding to a form of determinism (fate) and the latter holding to what might be termed a libertarian free will. The Pharisees—the largest and most influential group—hold the two in tension; but their stance should not be confused with a modern-day compatibilist view, which holds that "people are only free when they think, speak, and act in ways compatible with how God created them and decreed their lives to be."[11] Rather, "the Pharisees, fully aware that predestination precludes free-will, adopted a middle view, declaring that man is subject to predestination in his material life, but is completely free in his spiritual life."[12] Yet none of these groups, including the Essenes, hold to a hard determinism where all things are preordained; this concept is apparently foreign to Judaism.[13]

We see this similar dual belief throughout Scripture. We read about the hardening of Pharaoh's heart (Exod. 7), God's predestining us according to his good pleasure (Eph. 1:5), and about how "every decision is from the LORD" (Prov. 16:33). But we also read about God's giving the Ten Commandments (Exod. 20; Deut. 5), Moses's command to the people to follow the Lord (Deut. 30:11-20), Jesus's challenge to live out the heart of the kingdom (Matt. 5–7), and multiple other ethical and relational directives, which all presuppose the freedom and responsibility of the hearers. Therefore, while Scripture holds fate and free will in tension, we must shy away from reading these two as contradictory or applying modern-day constructs or definitions to Scripture.

As stated above, luck or chance fills the void between human choices and divine master plan (not to be confused with determinism); and thus, it is natural that we will find this phenomenon in Scripture, though usually indirectly.

The most direct reference comes in Ecclesiastes, a book that in many ways deals with some of the same frustrations and arbitrariness of life that we discuss here. The writer states:

I have seen something else under the sun:

> The race is not to the swift
>> or the battle to the strong,
> nor does food come to the wise
>> or wealth to the brilliant
>> or favor to the learned;
> but time and chance happen to them all.

Moreover, no one knows when their hour will come:

> As fish are caught in a cruel net,
>> or birds are taken in a snare,
> so people are trapped by evil times
>> that fall unexpectedly upon them. (Eccles. 9:11-12)

This rather bleak picture is a reminder that in this world, things do not appear to work the way we might expect. In frustration, the writer proclaims that "time and chance" happen to us all. In other words, even when we know and do all the right things, inevitably there will be times when evil falls unexpectedly upon us; there will be times of bad luck! Yet this picture, and the writer's pessimism (cf. 4:1-7) in general, may lead one to feel helpless and hopeless. For this reason, the writer reminds readers that we must recognize God's control and take life as it comes, both good and bad. Compare, for instance, his words in 7:13-14:

> Consider what God has done:
>
> Who can straighten
>
> what he has made crooked?
>
> When times are good, be happy;
>
> but when times are bad, consider this:
>
> God has made the one
>
> as well as the other.
>
> Therefore, no one can discover
>
> anything about their future.

As noted above, this should not be read as proof of hard determinism but, rather, as a frustrated recognition by the author that he does not have the answers and God does. Like many of the psalms, this is a lament, a crying out to God for answers, while simultaneously placing trust in this same God. As has already been stated, this God invites wrestling. God recognizes our frustration and invites us to cry out in the midst of it, especially during times of pain, persecution, injustice, and bad luck.

The book of Acts presents us with another account of luck. In Acts 1:12-26, we read about how the apostles go about choosing Judas Iscariot's replacement. Though the decision is not completely random, neither is it fully determined. They start by nominating two men, Joseph and Matthias, who have been with them for some time and who have been a witness to Jesus's ministry and resurrection (vv. 21-22). There is no doubt that both of these men are godly and equally qualified. Instead of just making a decision, we read, in verses 24-26:

Then they prayed, "Lord, you know everyone's heart. Show us which of these two you have chosen to take over this apostolic ministry, which Judas left to go where he belongs." Then they cast lots, and the lot fell to Matthias; so he was added to the eleven apostles.

Is Matthias's election by the casting of lots a form of luck? Casting lots is a common practice, as evidenced in the Old Testament. It is used to divide the land of Canaan among the tribes of Israel (Num. 26:52ff; Josh. 18:6); to select men for battle (Judg. 20:9-10); to elect Saul as king (1 Sam. 10:19ff); to determine priestly assignments (1 Chron. 24–26); to decide guilt (Jon. 1:7); to decide which goat is sacrificed on the Day of Atonement (Lev. 16); and for many other occasions.

Though common, the practice of casting lots is based on chance and speaks more to the players' perception and understanding of God than to any reality about God. In fact, William Beardslee has shown that this practice is relatively rare in postexilic Judaism. He writes:

On the whole the actual casting of lots played a small role in Hebrew and Jewish religious life, as is only natural in view of the strong element of responsibility in the confrontation of the holy which is characteristic both of the legal and of the prophetic apprehension of Yahweh. Naturally the casting of lots in secularized form existed in Hebrew and Jewish life. In Judaism, however, this practice seems to have been confined to relatively trivial or purely playful functions.[14]

Beardslee goes on to show how the casting of lots becomes more of a metaphor for a decision of God and is viewed as a present, gracious gift from God.[15]

So why do the apostles cast lots in Acts 1:26? Is it a ritualistic act in which they see God's will being disseminated, or is it a way of giving God the credit for selection? We argue the latter. Thus, the actual result of this gambling match is a matter of luck and, simultaneously, a way for the apostles to give God all the credit. They are comfortable with this decision because they have already done the responsible work of narrowing it down to two qualified candidates.

Both of these examples have dealt with more or less direct references to luck, but they are the exception. Rather, the more prevalent picture of luck in Scripture is found in the front of the text as we reason through how this relational God works in spite of human choices while not limiting them. We find a perfect example in the life of Joseph.

As we read the biblical story of Joseph (Gen. 37–50), we see his fall from favored son to slave to prisoner and then his dramatic rise to ruler. We are awestruck by how God intervenes along the way to fulfill the dreams he gave to Joseph at the beginning (37:5-11) and how Joseph recognizes and proclaims God's providence by the end:

> Don't be afraid. Am I in the place of God? You intended to harm me, but God intended it for good to accomplish what is now being done, the saving of many lives. So then, don't be afraid. I will provide for you and your children. (Gen. 50:19-21; cf. 45:4-9)

While these words are comforting, we should not immediately conclude that they depict a picture of reality in which God has manipulated all the events to bring about this particular conclusion. It is truer to recognize Joseph's statement as representing his personal reflection on what took place.[16] However, reading from this side of the events, we can see a larger picture in which God works in spite of the choices made along the way. This is an imperative stance; otherwise, we deal with more difficult questions with much deeper consequences.

Let's take a moment and evaluate the many human choices along the way that end in Joseph's rise to power. Jacob *chooses* to love Joseph more than his other sons (37:3), which makes Joseph's brothers hate him (v. 4). The brothers *choose* to be jealous to the point of nearly killing Joseph, then selling him into slavery (vv. 19-32). Potiphar's wife *chooses* to try to seduce Joseph, and when she fails, she *chooses* to lie to her husband about it, and Joseph winds up in prison (39:7-20).

These are just a few of the many sinful choices made along the way. If God is the one who orchestrated all these things, then not only has free will been removed, but moreover, God *made* his creation do evil and sinful things. Do the ends really justify the means?

If we are willing to agree that God does not *cause* these evil choices, then we can recognize that Joseph experiences a lot of bad luck along the way. However, God is still present and active in bringing about a way to offer redemption. Yet we must also recognize that Joseph still has to choose to do good, choose to have a positive attitude in the midst of his trials, choose to forgive his brothers, and choose to trust God.

Likewise, his brothers eventually have to choose to repent and choose to accept both Joseph and God's forgiveness.

Questions for Further Reflection or Small Group Discussion

1. When was the last time you prayed a prayer of desperation? How did God respond?

2. Have you ever felt you needed to defend God when you believed people were not giving God credit for an instance of divine intervention? Explain.

3. What do you think of the term *luck*? Do you think people who claim to be Christians can use the phrases *good luck* or *bad luck*?

4. When did you first come to see the complexities of the world in which we live? Do you see this complexity as a challenge or an opportunity?

5. What do you think of the decision-making practices of the apostles who both pray and cast lots?

6. Do you see the biblical story of Joseph and his brothers as more a vision of God's sovereign activity or of human choices?

7. Do you think God is in control of the world? What does that mean?

For Further Study

Beginner to Intermediate

Clapper, Gregory S. *When the World Breaks Your Heart: Spiritual Ways of Living with Tragedy.* Nashville: Upper Room Books, 1999.

Lodahl, Michael. *When Love Bends Down: Images of the Christ Who Meets Us Where We Are.* Kansas City: Beacon Hill Press of Kansas City, 2006.

Wright, Christopher J. H. *The God I Don't Understand: Reflections on Tough Questions of Faith.* Grand Rapids: Zondervan, 2008.

Yancey, Philip. *The Question That Never Goes Away.* Grand Rapids: Zondervan, 2014.

More Advanced

Bartholomew, David J. *God, Chance and Purpose: Can God Have It Both Ways?* Cambridge: Cambridge University Press, 2008.

Sanders, John. *The God Who Risks: A Theology of Providence.* Downers Grove, IL: InterVarsity Press, 1998.

Wright, N. T. *Evil and the Justice of God.* London: SPCK, 2006.

3

FATE, CHAOS, AND FAITH

• • •

Fate

Fate is a well-known concept that has been popularized and romanticized in our world by Hollywood films for decades. Fate is represented by the two lovers who are destined for each other; the protagonist who is preordained to meet a tragic end (usually to save the world); or the underdog whose life inescapably moves toward a fairy-tale, happily-ever-after ending.

Perhaps one of the best modern-day examples of the concept of fate is the movie *Slumdog Millionaire*.[1] The story revolves around a young man, Jamal Malik, who has grown up in the slums of Mumbai and has found himself one question away from winning the grand prize on the Indian version of *Who Wants to Be a Millionaire?* Prior to answering the final question, Jamal is arrested and detained on suspicion of cheating; everyone wants to know how it is possible for this young, poor, uneducated "slumdog" to have answered all these difficult questions correctly.

The majority of the movie is a series of flashbacks from Jamal's challenging life, which reveal how he knew each of the answers. The film depicts a concept of fate in which life has to have happened the way it did, with all its pains and struggles, or else Jamal would not be prepared for this pinnacle moment. His life is not by chance, nor are the game show questions a matter of luck; rather, everything has happened for a reason, and only in the present moment has that reality become clear.

In Greek mythology, fate is described as a three-person figure named *Moirai* (or Moirae). This trio of goddesses is tasked with determining the fate of every mortal being. The first goddess (*Clotho*, meaning "spinner") spins the thread of life, determining when and where a person will be born. The second (*Lachesis*, meaning "apportioner of lots") determines the length of the thread and, thus, a person's lifespan. The third (*Atropos*, meaning "she who cannot be turned") is to cut the thread at the end of one's days; she determines the manner in which a person dies.[2]

Many today view life in this same, fated way. People believe we are on a preplanned journey in which everything has already been decided, including when and how we die. They say things such as, "When it's my time, it's just my time; no one can do anything about it," or "It's just part of my destiny." Some people assume fate to be a secular idea, unrelated to the Christian faith. Yet the concepts tied to fate are nearly identical to those found in the Christian understanding of God's providence,[3] or in what we have called a theology of certainty. The only difference is possibly the person or thing to which this fate is attributed.

For instance, Wayne Oates, in his work *Luck: A Secular Faith*, suggests that there are two options in regard to the givenness of life. Either a person can believe in divine providence (the "sacred option") or in luck (the "secular option"), which he defines as confidence or faith in fate.[4] For Oates, luck as a secular faith suggests that we approach life as self-sufficient, trusting in our own skill to calculate the odds in order to triumph over whatever happens.[5] He describes gambling as the key modern example, since it is focused on the present rather than the eternal and since it is dependent on human action apart from divine intervention. He suggests that "calculating the probabilities is a secularized form of providence,"[6] which replaces responsibility. While fatalism (the assumption that one has no control over what happens in life) is left with chance, Christian faith, on the other hand, has divine providence.[7]

Yet, in reading Oates's book, it becomes evident that the only real difference between these two views is that one believes in divine fate and the other believes in some form of luck, which is depicted as a kind of secular fate. It is not enough to replace the secular option with an identical divine option. However, the God of relationship we have been speaking of does not deem it necessary to control humanity and, therefore, has not fated us.

We should also note that the luck Oates speaks about is not at all similar to what was spoken of in chapter 2. Oates's understanding of luck as some sort of godlike entity that is worshipped by the secular world is what we might deem a belief in magic or superstition (more in chapter 4). We do not think luck should be worshipped or even sought after by way of some superstitious act. Rather, we view luck as an inevitable part of the free will/free grace, relational system God has created and that, rather than seeking luck out, it usually finds us.

Chaos

Harold Kushner's classic work, *When Bad Things Happen to Good People*, deals with the reality that tragedies occur in our world even when we least expect them and even to people who do not deserve them. For Kushner, our response is what is most important. Too often, when tragedies strike, we expend a lot of time and energy seeking someone to blame; we blame ourselves, we blame someone else, and we even blame God. This is understandable for those who hold to a deterministic framework in which God is in control and everything happens for a reason. However, Kushner suggests a different reality:

> The world is mostly an orderly, predictable place, showing ample evidence of God's thoroughness and handiwork, but pockets of chaos remain. Most of the time, the events of the universe follow firm natural laws. But every now and then, things happen not contrary to those laws of nature but outside them. Things happen which could just as easily have happened differently.[8]

In a world where new tragedies occur daily, is it possible we have extended the blame game too far? Would we not do better to take seriously what Kushner terms the "pockets of chaos" that exist beyond the realm of deterministic fate and God's willful providence? Would it not be more helpful, in the midst of the chaos, to cling tightly to the God who subdues the chaos?

Both chaos and God's subduing of chaos are pictures seen throughout Scripture. In fact, the Bible opens with this story in Genesis 1:1-2:

In the beginning God created the heavens and the earth. Now the earth was formless and empty, darkness was over the surface of the deep, and the Spirit of God was hovering over the waters.

While many of us might jump past the opening words of the creation story and focus on the peaceful, perfect paradise that is the garden of Eden, this is not how the story begins. The opening setting is a lot less like lounging midday in the sands of Hawaii and more like being dropped at midnight into the center of the Atlantic. Empty. Formless. Darkness. Chaos! It is far from peaceful and far from perfect.

But then we read that next line: "and the Spirit of God was hovering over the waters." And with these words, suddenly everything changes. We discover that we are not alone in the chaos. God is there to conquer the dark, chaotic waters that pervade this space. The creation story does not detail an eternally peaceful paradise but describes a God who gives boundaries and form to an otherwise perilous, dangerous place. It is this God, the God who hovers over the chaos, who has the power to bring life into the emptiness simply by speaking words.

LIGHT. SKY. LAND. SUN. FLIGHT. TORTOISES. KIWIS. KITTENS. US.

GOOD. GOOD. GOOD. GOOD. GOOD. VERY GOOD!

The God who hovers over the deep waters brings light in the midst of darkness, stability in the midst of chaos. However, the chaos is not destroyed (at least, not yet); it is simply contained (for now). As Paul Tillich reminds us, "Creation and chaos belong to each other, and even the exclusive monotheism of biblical religion confirms this structure of life."[9]

Even though God contained this chaos, sin unleashed it again. The presence of the potency of water throughout the biblical narratives, from global floods to raging rivers, reminds us at every turn that chaos is still very real and very present. In fact, water is often synonymous with chaos in the biblical narrative, which is why the glorious picture of the new heaven and new earth described in Revelation 21:1 includes the words "and there was no longer any sea."

This vision of water as chaos makes the Genesis account of Noah more intriguing. The utter sinfulness of humanity has allowed the chaos to reenter the story (Gen. 6:5). The Bible speaks of God being grieved so deeply that he allows creation to be consumed by the waters of chaos (vv. 6ff). But this water is not just from above, in the form of rain. Rather, we are told that "all the springs of the great deep burst forth, and the floodgates of the heavens were opened" (7:11). It is as if the waters of chaos, once held at bay by God, are released, re-forming a precreation chaos.

But chaos is never the end of the story. Instead, we read about God drying up the land, bringing form to formlessness, and calling Noah and all the animals out of the ark "so they can multiply on the earth and be fruitful and increase in number on it" (8:16-17; cf. 1:28). It is a re-creation story! God once again invites humanity to join him in the work of creation and in subduing the chaos through an authentic faith relationship with him and with the rest of creation.

We see this story repeated in many ways throughout Scripture; from the crossing of the Red Sea to the crossing of the Jordan, God invites us to trustfully and faithfully walk with God in the midst of the chaos of rising waters. Maybe the clearest picture of this invitation comes in the Gospels, when Jesus and his followers encounter a violent storm as they try to cross the Sea of Galilee (Matt. 8:23-27; Mark 4:35-41; Luke 8:22-25).

While the disciples desperately hold on for dear life, their master sleeps like a baby in the bottom of the boat. Afraid for their lives, they wake Jesus, who proceeds to rebuke the wind and calm the waves. In fear and amazement, the disciples ask, "Who is this? Even the wind and the waves obey him" (Mark 4:41). Here we see God hovering over the waters once again. While the disciples have trouble understanding how their Divine Leader can be so calm in the midst of the turbulent waters, Jesus knows that the wind and waves are part of the journey.

God is the awesome Creator who subdues the chaos of our world. However, the world in which God placed us was never a completely safe place of absolutes and certainty; it has always been a place of potentiality and peril because it is a place of relationship and love and human choice. It has always been a place where obedience and fidelity are essential to the continuation of order and peace, to keeping the chaos at bay. In fact, chaos is the natural result of human disobedience and un-participation in God's ways of being in the world.

There is evidence of the uncertainty and chaos in our world everywhere. Constant change and instability are part of the realities of the creation we inhabit. But as we look back at the story of God creating, we can be assured that the chaos is nothing God has not encountered and conquered before. We must always remember that the God who can bring form to formlessness offers a world where certainty may not have been its foundation, but certainty is still its future.

Therefore, any theology worth its weight must be broad enough not to require the absolutism of fate; it must be open to the risk of learning to live a life of faith in the chaos. A theology of luck shapes a worldview that makes it possible to move from fate—through chaos—to faith. Our finally freed God is no longer bound to be the only potent responsible party in the universe; instead, we have a shared vision for partnering in faith in a world of varied responsibilities.

As Jürgen Moltmann suggests, a god who is known only by the ability to control things is hardly a god worth following, and certainly not a description of the God who made himself known in Jesus of Nazareth.[10] Our God calls us to a relationship of love and not fear (1 John 4:18). The God who is present in our chaos and who guides us toward his future is the God who is worthy of our faith.

Faith

Faith in God is not acquiescence to the desires of a totalitarian dictator; it is participation in the reign of a benevolent king. It is dynamic because relationship is dynamic, especially when this relationship is with God. Those accustomed to a deterministic God may find this kind of faith unsettling.

Though we might be more comfortable with a faith that allows us to sit back and praise God during the good times and blame God during the bad times, this type of faith does not usually last because it does not satisfy. We were not created for this type of passive, distant, and sterile nonrelationship. We were created for an intimate, active, and sometimes aggressive wrestling match between the Creator and his creation; we were created to love, and love gets messy. If you do not believe us, take a look at the cross.

The biblical story of Jacob (Gen. 25:19–35:29), son of Isaac and Rebekah, twin brother of Esau, is a fascinating picture of this kind of faith, which has enormous bearings for the people of God well past the Genesis narratives. Most of us know the basics of Jacob's story. He is born clutching his older brother's heel, and his name means something like "deceiver" or "cheater." He lives up to this name and cheats his brother out of his birthright and, later, tricks his father into giving him Esau's blessing. He then runs and hides from Esau because he fears for his life.

When we pick up the story in Genesis 32, Jacob is married to Leah and Rachel, has eleven children, has amassed a great amount of wealth, and is preparing to meet Esau for the first time since cheating him out of his blessing. The narrative climaxes at this very point. What will happen next? Will Esau seek revenge? Has Jacob changed? Are God's covenant promises through Jacob still on track? Then comes the encounter before the encounter.

We are told of a wrestling match between Jacob and "a man" who is later revealed to be God (vv. 22-30). In the course of this struggle, we see a change take place in Jacob. The old Jacob constantly ran from danger and always looked out for himself and his interests. However, the new Jacob, even when given opportunity to escape, holds on—not for dear life but for blessing. Why? What does blessing mean if he does not have his life?

When we think of blessing, we think of family, health, and fortune, but Jacob already has these things. In fact, he is at risk of losing them during this wrestling match. Some have suggested the blessing Jacob seeks is God's protection from Esau. We do not think this is the case. Jacob seems prepared to die at the hands of this "man," so survival does not appear to be the motivating factor. Instead, Jacob has come to the end of a long life of deception, cheating, and self-preservation. The blessing he seeks is to be released from himself and to embrace a life truly reliant on God, whether in life or in death.

"What is your name?" asks the man (v. 27). Immediately we are taken back to Genesis 27 and Jacob's first blessing. However, there is a marked difference. The first blessing by Isaac came through deception; when asked who he was, Jacob answered, "Esau." No doubt, this lie has haunted him many times throughout his life. No doubt, this false claim is fresh on his mind as he prepares to meet his brother, Esau. Now is the moment of truth. Now is the moment of redemption. Now is the moment for Jacob to embrace who he is and who he has always been.

"What is your name?" I am Jacob! I am the cheater! The deceiver! The prodigal son!

God knows Jacob needs to come to terms with who he really is, needs to admit it to himself. Jacob needs to come to a place where he is finally ready to admit he cannot do it on his own and every past attempt has ultimately failed. Numerous times he has claimed he wants to follow God but has constantly chosen his own path. Here God allows him to wrestle—with himself, with who he is, with who he will be moving forward, with God. "What is your name?"

"You shall no longer be called Jacob, but Israel, for you have striven with God and with humans, and have prevailed" (32:28, NRSV).

This is the kind of faith we are talking about! This is the kind of faith God invites us to! Not a passive acceptance of our lot in life, but a striving with God, a moving past our embrace of worldly conformity to a life of transformation in which we embrace a dynamic relationship with the God of creation and redemption. God invites us to wrestle with him!

Jacob's story is seen throughout Scripture, and these stories call us to the same kind of relationship with God. Take Moses, for example. Moses often wrestles with God, and usually in situations you would not think were appropriate. In Exodus chapters 3 and 4, we read about Moses's calling. It is a rather odd interaction that does not paint Moses in a very positive light. In fact, some argue that God does not come off looking very good either.

God appears to Moses in a burning bush and verbally calls Moses to lead the people of Israel out of Egypt and into the

Promised Land. Right away we can recognize that this is neither the passive god of deism or the controlling god of determinism. If he were the former, he would not engage humanity; if the latter, he would not give humanity the opportunity to challenge the request.

And challenge the request is exactly what Moses does. The almighty Creator of the universe appears to him and commands him to do something, and he comes up with a series of excuses for why he is not the right person for the job. What kind of God is this? Why doesn't God just force him to do what he wants? Why doesn't God choose someone who won't question the decision? The narrative presents a patient and compliant God. God is willing to allow Moses room for questions, room for doubt, and room for wrestling. God answers every one of Moses's concerns and is even willing to change his plans to help Moses answer positively. For many, this does not sound like a very impressive God. Why should an all-powerful Deity yield to the will of a mere human?

In Exodus 32, we read about another encounter between Moses and God. While Moses is on Mount Sinai receiving the Ten Commandments from the Lord, the people of Israel grow impatient and have Aaron build them a golden calf to worship. We are told that God burns with anger against them and informs Moses of Israel's actions and of his plan to destroy them and to make a new people through Moses. But this is not the end of the story. Moses has been through a lot with these people and is not willing to let God off the hook so easily. Instead, he wrestles with God over this situation, and God acquiesces.

Moses is willing to challenge God, and God is willing to listen to Moses. Yes, this speaks to the courage of Moses as a leader and to his love for the Israelite people. However, it speaks even more to an intimacy between Moses and God that most of us would not dare assume we could ever have and that many would not even want if they knew they could have. It speaks of a God who is confident enough in who he is and in his own power to allow inferior humanity to engage him at this level. It speaks to a genuine relationship, to which God has invited us. It speaks of love!

The book of Job is a final example. It is a greatly misunderstood and misinterpreted book that some find comforting and others, reprehensible. If we are to understand the book of Job for what it was intended, we must begin by understanding its literary genre. Many read this book as a narrative because it follows many of the standard devices for this genre such as character, plot, conflict, and resolution. However, it also includes large sections of Hebrew poetry and is in fact understood as wisdom literature, which means it should be read with the same mentality as one would read Psalms, Proverbs, and Ecclesiastes as opposed to how one would read Genesis, Exodus, and Deuteronomy.

So what is the wisdom to be found in this book? Is it that God is sovereign and wise, and humanity lacks understanding? Is it that we should not question or doubt God's purposes? Is it that we can be righteous in the midst of our suffering? Yes and no. These do not fully encompass the message of wisdom found in Job.

Yes, God is sovereign, a fact made clear in both the opening and closing chapters. However, this sovereign God is also clearly not the cause of Job's suffering. And though Job clearly lacks understanding, this God is patient and forgiving toward him. In fact, if Job teaches us anything, it is that God allows us to doubt, to question, and to be angry in the midst of our suffering. Job believes his suffering is from God; he is wrong. Job buys into the cultural norms of his day, which say that the righteous are rewarded and the unrighteous punished. However, Job knows he is righteous and therefore believes God to be acting unjustly.

I loathe my very life;

therefore I will give free rein to my complaint

and speak out in the bitterness of my soul.

I say to God: Do not declare me guilty,

but tell me what charges you have against me. Does it please you to oppress me,

to spurn the work of your hands,

while you smile on the plans of the wicked? (Job 10:1-3)

• • •

God has turned me over to the ungodly

and thrown me into the clutches of the wicked.

All was well with me, but he shattered me;

he seized me by the neck and crushed me.

He has made me his target;

his archers surround me.

Without pity, he pierces my kidneys

and spills my gall on the ground.

Again and again he bursts upon me;

he rushes at me like a warrior.
I have sewed sackcloth over my skin
    and buried my brow in the dust.
My face is red with weeping,
    dark shadows ring my eyes;
yet my hands have been free of violence
    and my prayer is pure. (16:11-17)

When reading passages like these, the question of Job's innocence comes to mind. How are Job's words different from those of his friends? Do not both groups misunderstand and misrepresent God? In fact, many see Job's words as blasphemous.

However, when God reenters the story (chaps. 38–41), he does not come with condemnation but with grace. God challenges Job's thinking while never fully answering Job's complaints. In the end, Job is vindicated, and his friends are rebuked because Job is willing to wrestle with God. Even in his ignorance, Job's faith is strong enough to challenge and question God. Unlike the faith of Job's wife, who abandons God when trials come (2:9), and unlike the faith of Job's friends, who are not willing to move beyond their own rigid structures and actually engage God, Job's faith demands interaction—because Job has a dynamic relationship with God and not merely a stagnant knowledge.

Love engages! Love fights for the one it believes in, which sometimes means fighting *with* this one. God invites this kind of engagement with a listening ear and gentle, gracious correction—but only if we are willing to listen and only if we are willing to stick around long enough to hear him. Moreover, like Job, when God does correct us, we, too, must be willing to repent (42:1-6).

A faithful relationship with God will certainly not be mistaken for a sedentary life. Instead, a healthy life of faith can be characterized by struggling and questioning God. Throughout the stories of Scripture, we see God's followers embraced by God despite not having all their questions resolved. A theology of luck allows us the space to wrestle with this same God. God is looking for persons to wrestle with, to love; God is looking for those who will participate in God's movement in the world.

Questions for Further Reflection or Small Group Discussion

1. What comes to mind when you hear the word *fate*? Have you ever thought about the relationship between God and fate?

2. What things do you hear people describe in terms of fate in our society?

3. What do you think Rabbi Kushner means by the term "pockets of chaos"? Do you agree or disagree?

4. What did you think of the vision presented of Genesis 1? Have you ever thought about the relationship between creation and chaos?

5. What do you think of the idea of God "being free from being the only potent responsible party in the universe"?

6. React to this definition of faith: "Faith in God is not acquiescence to the desires of a totalitarian dictator; it is participation in the reign of a benevolent king."

7. When have you wrestled with God? Do you think wrestling with God is a sign of health or disrespect?

For Further Study

Beginner to Intermediate

Gundry, Stanley N., and Dennis W. Jowers, eds. *Four Views on Divine Providence*. Grand Rapids: Zondervan, 2011.

Kushner, Harold. *When Bad Things Happen to Good People*. 12th ed. New York: Shocken Books, 2001.

McKnight, Scot. *A Long Faithfulness: The Case for Christian Perseverance*. Colorado Springs: Patheos Press, 2013.

More Advanced

Fretheim, Terence E. *The Pentateuch*. Nashville: Abingdon Press, 1996.

Goldingay, John. *Key Questions about Christian Faith: Old Testament Answers*. Grand Rapids: Baker Academic, 2010.

Moltmann, Jürgen. *The Crucified God: The Cross of Christ as the Foundation and Criticism of Christian Theology*. London: SCM Press, 1974.

THE MOVEMENT FROM MAGIC TO MYSTERY

○ ○ ○

How is God active in the world?

What is our place in this world?

4
ABRACADABRA, HOCUS-POCUS

• • •

A Manipulable God?

Most of us have some experience playing with toy claw machines. They draw us in with their big claws and big prizes by appealing to our big egos that are convinced we can beat the game even though so many others have failed. We insert dollar after dollar and grow more and more frustrated as we fail to obtain the prize we want. Some people are disciplined enough to walk away after a couple of unsuccessful attempts. However, some grow obsessed, thinking they must be doing something wrong and that they can correct whatever it is. They carry on, trying new ways to manipulate the machine, repeating useless chants, even becoming violent with the machine. Frustration mounts, but they all eventually walk away, some successful and others defeated.

Similarly, many view their God as a kind of giant toy claw machine. This God is not controlling but controlled; not passive but often ignored; definitely not loving, though many have fallen in love with this kind of fictional God. We call this God the manipulable God. It is actually no God at all but, rather, the invention of those who themselves want to be God.

The cultures of the ancient Near East had many manipulable gods and even more magicians and diviners tasked with trying to move these various gods toward a particular action or outcome. Witchcraft, astrology, reading entrails, self-mutilation, animal sacrifices, and even infant sacrifices were all common practices used to interpret the various gods' wills and to control or appease them.[1]

However, Israel's God, Yahweh, is not like these foreign gods, and his people are explicitly called to denounce such pagan practices. Yahweh is too powerful to be manipulated by human concoctions. He wants a relationship with humanity rather than an exchange of meaningless actions (see Isa. 1:11-14). He desires for his people to trust him and to come to him for revelation and insight. In addition, since God finds these pagan actions detestable, he desires to partner with Israel in revealing the folly of these practices to the other nations. This is why many of the Old Testament stories show the superiority of Yahweh and his people over that of the other gods and their practitioners.

Scholars have suggested that the ten plagues in Exodus 7:14–12:30 each correspond to a different Egyptian deity (see accompanying chart). Indeed, many of these connections seem possible if not probable, especially in the light of Exodus 12:12, where the Lord declares: "I will bring judgment on all the gods of Egypt. I am the Lord." Furthermore, Pharaoh has many wise men and sorcerers (also called magicians) who are able to replicate some of the signs and plagues (7:11-12, 22; 8:7), but they eventually admit that Moses's God is too strong (8:18-19).

PLAGUES	EGYPTIAN GODS[2]
1. blood	Hapi, god of the Nile, bringer of fertility
2. frogs	Hek/Heqt, frog-headed goddess of fruitfulness
3. gnats	Geb, earth god
4. flies	Kheper(a), in the form of a beetle
5. livestock	Hathor/Khnum, cow-headed goddess/ram-headed god
6. boils	Sekhmet, plague and healing goddess
7. hail	Nut, goddess of the sky
8. locusts	Serapia, protector from locusts
9. darkness	Re/Ra, sun god and king of the gods
10. death of firstborn	Taurt, goddess of maternity

First Kings 18 is another great example of the contrast between Yahweh and manipulable gods. King Ahab, ruler of the northern kingdom, has failed his people by allowing his wife Jezebel to corrupt Israel's worship and murder the Lord's prophets (v. 4). Elijah, the prophet of Yahweh, confronts Ahab: "You have abandoned the Lord's commands and have followed the Baals" (v. 18). Baal, the Canaanite storm and fertility god, is popular in a dry land that is dependent on rain for fertility,[3] which makes the story even more interesting since we are told there is an extreme famine (v. 2) as a result of Yahweh stopping the rain for three and a half years (17:1; 18:1).

The stage is set for a showdown between Elijah's God and Ahab and Jezebel's god. Elijah sets up a contest on Mount Carmel in which he will face off against the 450 prophets of Baal to show whose god is more powerful. The task is simple: Each party will prepare a bull for sacrifice and place it on a pile of wood. They will then call upon their god, who is to answer by consuming the offering in flames. Elijah allows the prophets of Baal to go first, but despite all their efforts, prayers, screams, dancing, and even self-mutilation, Baal does not answer.

When it is Elijah's turn, he not only prepares the sacrifice but also digs a trench around it and drenches it with twelve large jars of water until "the water ran down around the altar and even filled the trench" (18:35). As one scholar put it, Elijah "was playing for the highest of stakes, and he made the conditions so unfavorable for himself that success would be not merely impressive but awesome."[4] Elijah prays that God will intervene and burn up the animal sacrifice, and "then the fire of the LORD fell and burned up the sacrifice, the wood, the stones and the soil, and also licked up the water in the trench" (v. 38). Baal is discredited, his prophets are destroyed, and the God of Israel is exalted.

Notice the difference between Elijah's faith and that of the false prophets of Baal. Elijah's actions are the fulfillment of revelations given to him from his God. He has walked in relationship with Yahweh and trusts him to be present. The prophets of Baal have no such relationship with their god. Their faith is based on magic, superstitions, and manipulation, and it fails when it is most needed.

As we know, even Israel falls prey to these kinds of attempts to manipulate God. For instance, in Isaiah 1, we learn of God's anger against his people because they move through the motions of worship while simultaneously doing all kinds of evil against God.

"The multitude of your sacrifices—
what are they to me?" says the LORD.
"I have more than enough of burnt offerings,
of rams and the fat of fattened animals;
I have no pleasure
in the blood of bulls and lambs and goats.
When you come to appear before me,
who has asked this of you,
this trampling of my courts?
Stop bringing meaningless offerings!
Your incense is detestable to me.
New Moons, Sabbaths and convocations—
I cannot bear your worthless assemblies.
Your New Moon feasts and your appointed festivals
I hate with all my being.
They have become a burden to me;
I am weary of bearing them.
When you spread out your hands in prayer,
I hide my eyes from you;
even when you offer many prayers,
I am not listening." (Vv. 11-15)

These are some harsh words, yet they give us a picture of God's desire for authentic relationship with his people. These very acts of worship that God requested of his people in Leviticus are now no better than the pagan practices of the prophets of Baal because they are both attempts to manipulate. Israel's religious rituals have become actions meant to appease God so

God will overlook their sin; they are meant to elicit a particular positive action on God's part. They are not actually worshipping God, because their motivation is not love or relationship but selfish gain. We, too, are reminded that our God cannot be manipulated or controlled, and therefore, if we desire true relationship with this God and desire to offer true worship to this God, then our faith and actions must look very different.

Magic-Minded Faith

In the 2009 film *The Invention of Lying*,[5] Ricky Gervais plays a down-on-his-luck bachelor looking to turn his life around. However, Gervais's character, Mark, lives in an alternative reality where everyone is brutally honest, incapable of lying, and unable to doubt. In his world, the odds are stacked against those who have not won the gene-pool lottery. The less attractive and less gifted people, like Mark, have trouble succeeding in life because no one has the ability to do anything but live out of the truth as they see it.

That is, until Mark tells the first lie ever, and it works. Mark's newfound power of lying is first used for selfish gain and, later, to help others. At one point, Mark creates the concept of an afterlife to comfort his mother on her deathbed. This lie gets out of hand, and Mark is forced to extend it, creating the idea of a "Man in the Sky" who controls all things and gives rewards to those who are good. Mark's story spreads, and he becomes incredibly famous for bringing peace and comfort to those in need.

While many Christians view this movie as an attempt to discredit their faith, we want to highlight an ironic truth about the faith of those in the movie, a faith that needs to be discredited. Many Christians believe in the type of functional God depicted in the film. Like the movie, their faith in God is fictional because it really is not faith in God but faith in heaven, some type of reward, or an escape from something. It is often motivated by fear and selfishness. This kind of faith is forced to construct a God it can control.

We think we can manipulate God, either for our own selfish gain or for some noble purpose. We think that if we go to church often enough or give enough money, then God will bless us. We think that if we pray the right words and do the right things, then God will give us what we want. In the words of Chris Lautsbaugh:

> We take the form of a magician, concocting a magic potion. A bit of faith, sprinkle in some prayer, and a pinch of fasting. Stir it all together, say the magic words, and "poof"—you get what you are hoping for.[6]

This manipulation can take on several forms from superstitious practices to false religiosity to genuine but misplaced faith. While most Christians would verbally deny any reliance on magic or superstitions, their actions often look no different from the prophets of Baal. Like biblical Israel, we, too, are prone to assimilate our faith practices with those of the dominant cultures around us.

In a survey taken of churchgoers in the United Kingdom, it was recorded that almost half of those surveyed (47 percent) believed in the power of certain rituals and actions to determine significant outcomes in their lives. Some of these rites included finding a four-leaf clover, hanging up a horseshoe, or avoiding opening an umbrella indoors.[7] This same group of churchgoers also admitted to participating in some type of "luck-related behavior." In fact, more than three-fourths of those surveyed said they had occasionally practiced crossing their fingers (80 percent), knocking on wood (79 percent), throwing spilled salt over their shoulders (73 percent), and throwing a coin into a wishing well (73 percent) in order to bring about good luck.[8]

What moves us to this kind of magic-minded, superstitious faith? Is it our view of God? Do we view God as manipulable? Or is it that we do not really fully trust this God—that we're just hedging our bets? Of course, some believe themselves to be way too spiritual to rely on such superstitions. Some prefer more religious forms of manipulation. For instance, at one time or another most Christians have probably practiced bibliomancy,[9] the exercise of randomly opening the Bible and pointing to a passage of Scripture in order to understand God's will for a particular situation or to predict the future. Is this really faith? Or is this an attempt to force God to give us an answer when we want it?

Like Isaiah 1, many of us have moved through the religious motions in search of some magical blessing from God. For the less religious, attending Christmas and Easter services is hopefully enough to appease God for another year. For those more devoted, or at least more conscious of their own sinfulness, going to church once a week, reading Scripture occasionally, or praying daily is a way of fulfilling their part of the religious contract. We are not trying to be cynical, but we do want to make one thing very clear: If a person's faith is only a transaction of his or her religious actions for God's blessing, then it is not a relationship; it is manipulation!

We do not suggest that all Christians seek this kind of sterile exchange between themselves and God. Many Christians have a genuine desire for an authentic relationship with God but have been caught up in the consumerism of our culture, which has so infiltrated every aspect of our lives that we actually think a genuine relationship is a transaction. "If I give you something, you must give me something in return." This is all well and fine when each party's action is motivated by love, but what happens when one party starts to do something just to get a particular response or action in return? It has now moved from love to manipulation. This is often how our relationship with God works. It begins with genuine love but slowly becomes about selfish expectations, which inevitably lead to disappointment and, eventually, separation.

There are several stories in Scripture about this kind of manipulative relationship. For instance, Israel's wandering in the wilderness for forty years is mostly about the people's misconception of who this God is and their misplaced expectations of what he is supposed to do for them.

The book of Exodus is really about the people learning to understand who this God is and who he is not. These people have been in Egypt so long that they have adopted many of the native Egyptians' customs and beliefs. Their understanding of what a god is and how a person interacts with such a god is largely based on what they have seen and learned from the Egyptians. Gods are supposed to protect and provide; followers are supposed to offer sacrifices and worship idols. This system appears to work fine in Egypt, where they have houses and food and some semblance of stability and safety (yes, even in the midst of their slavery).

However, when they move into the wilderness, they also move into a completely new level of relationship with this God—a level that demands trust. They can no longer make meaningless sacrifices and move on with the day. They can no longer ignore this God when he does not deliver what they want. They cannot manipulate this God, but that does not stop them from trying. They try grumbling and complaining (Exod. 14:11-12; 16:1-3); they try saying and doing the right things (19:7-15); they try distancing themselves from this God (20:18-21); and they try making a new god to worship (32:1-6).

However, all these attempts ultimately fail, and they are left with a choice. Either they can continue to move forward with their false expectations of a manipulable God and, therefore, continue to wander aimlessly in the wilderness, or they can relinquish these selfish expectations and embrace a dynamic relationship with Yahweh in the Promised Land.

In the New Testament, Jesus also experiences false expectations and attempts at manipulation from most people, including those closest to him. The story of John the Baptist is one of the most fascinating. In Matthew 3:13-17, there can be no doubt that John believes Jesus was the long-awaited Messiah. John's belief is confirmed after Jesus's baptism when the heavens open and the Spirit descends on him like a dove "and a voice from heaven said, 'This is my Son, whom I love; with him I am well pleased'" (v. 17).

But only a few chapters later, as John sits in prison facing imminent death, we read about John sending his disciples to Jesus to ask, "Are you the one who is to come, or should we expect someone else?" (11:3). What happened to John's faith in this short period? Expectations happened. Like many of his time, John expects the Messiah to bring salvation to the righteous and judgment to the unrighteous. In fact, this is at the heart of the message John has been preaching:

> I baptize you with water for repentance. But after me comes one who is more powerful than I, whose sandals I am not worthy to carry. He will baptize you with the Holy Spirit and fire. His winnowing fork is in his hand, and he will clear his threshing floor, gathering his wheat into the barn and burning up the chaff with unquenchable fire. (Matt. 3:11-12)

From John's perspective, Jesus is not doing what he is supposed to be doing. He is not living up to John's expectations, so John tries to guide him in the right direction.

A similar episode happens with Peter when Jesus explains to his disciples how he must suffer, be rejected, and eventually die before rising again on the third day. We are told that Peter actually takes Jesus aside and rebukes him (Mark 8:31-32). How presumptuous, how bold both John and Peter are. They allow their expectations to overtake them and try to force Jesus into their mold.

Many of us have done this same thing. We think we know how God should act. We think our plan is better. We think if God would only listen to us, then everything would work out so much better. This is not how relationships work, or at least, it's not how they should work. Maybe it is not God who must change but our expectations of God. Maybe this is true of all our relationships. What would happen if we let go of our selfish expectations and just entered into the mystery of love? Just as the loving God cannot try to control us or coerce us into loving him, those who desire relationship with God must also abandon manipulation of all forms. They must move into the place of presence and trust. They must move away from selfish expectations and toward the mystery of love.

The Myth of Inadequate Faith

Another problem for those seeking genuine relationship with God is the myth of inadequate faith. This is tied to our consumerist understanding of relationship, but rather than thinking God is not living up to God's end of the bargain, we think the problem is our own. Someone has fed us the lie that God wants to give us what we ask but cannot or will not because we do not have enough faith. Much of the misunderstanding stems from a misreading of passages such as Matthew 17:20: "Truly I tell you, if you have faith as small as a mustard seed, you can say to this mountain, 'Move from here to there,' and it will move. Nothing will be impossible for you."

This statement is not primarily about the amount of faith a person has but, rather, about the object of a person's faith. Christ must be the focus of our faith, or it will not matter how much faith we have; it will still be ineffective. As Michael Wilkins writes regarding this passage:

Faith is not a particular substance, the more of which the disciples have, the more they can accomplish. It is not a gift of magic that can be manipulated at will. Rather, faith is confidence that we can do what God calls us to do—it is "taking God at his word." Therefore, the disciples should not place confidence in what they have but have confidence that if God calls them to do something, they can do it in his strength.[10]

Notice the difference. One type of faith focuses on ourselves and what we can do, and the other focuses on God and what God is doing. The misinterpretation arises from an overly myopic reading of Scripture. If the Bible is all about me and what God wants to do in and through me, then faith is obviously also about me. Right? Wrong! Scripture is about God. It is God's story, about God's love, God's righteousness, and God's faithfulness. Scripture invites us to participate in the faithfulness of Christ[11] rather than to have our own perfect faith, apart from God.

Mark 9:14-29 is another passage used to extend the myth of inadequate faith. The story recounts Jesus's healing of a demon-possessed boy after failed attempts by the disciples. Before the miracle, there is an interchange between the boy's father and Jesus in which the father asks Jesus if there is anything Jesus can do. Jesus replies, "Everything is possible for one who believes" (v. 23). To which the father responds, "I do believe; help me overcome my unbelief" (v. 24).

At first glance, Jesus appears to be making a connection between faith and healing in this passage. Yet, if this is the case, we can immediately rule out the degree-of-faith hypothesis, since Jesus heals the boy despite the father's acknowledgment of unbelief. In actuality, this passage has little to do with the father's or the son's faith but, rather, is focused on Jesus's authority. The disciples' failed attempts to exorcise this demon are a result of their misplaced faith in their own abilities, as evidenced by their lack of prayer (vv. 28-29).

As Kent Brower writes:

Prayer is not a technique, but a symbol of their [the disciples'] derived authority. It always signals faithful and utter dependence of the petitioner on divine authority.[12]

Faith is not so much about belief as it is about trust. The Greek noun *pistis* and verb *pisteuō* can be translated as "faith"/"belief" and "believe," respectively. They can also be translated as "trust" (which not only is a noun and a verb but also carries both concepts of "faith" and "belief"). We have tended to relegate faith and belief to the realm of intellectual knowledge, but the biblical understanding has more to do with commitment. In other words, it is not simply understanding but obedience! There is a wonderful word picture in the Greek words for "obedience" and "disobedience" that highlights the aspect of faith we are talking about. The root of both of these words is the Greek word *akouein*, which means "to hear." "Obedience" is *hypakoē*, which can literally be translated "hearing under," and "disobedience" is *parakoē*, which can literally be translated "hearing besides." Thus, obedience is the act of hearing God from the position of one who is under God, thus submitting to God's authority; whereas disobedience is the act of hearing God as one beside, thus as an equal.

If we truly trust God, we will have no problem submitting to God's authority, which will in no way take away from the relationship; in fact, it is the beginning of our side of the relationship. Authentic faith is a dependence upon God that is not reliant on the amount of faith we have but, rather, the focus of our faith. We cannot manipulate God with our faith, no matter how great our faith is. Likewise, God's love for us is not dependent upon our faith, no matter how small our faith is.

Questions for Further Reflection or Small Group Discussion

1. Have you ever thought of God as a giant toy claw machine? What are the ways we try to manipulate God? What are the things people try to manipulate God into doing?

2. What do you think the defeat of the Egyptian gods during the time of Moses and the defeat of the prophets of Baal during the time of Elijah says about the God of Israel? How do you think they feel when witnessing these events?

3. React to this quote: "If a person's faith is only a transaction of his or her religious actions for God's blessing, then it is not a relationship; it is manipulation!"

4. What "magic-minded, superstitious faith" have you experienced people participating in or have you participated in yourself?

5. When was the last time you sensed that you were going through religious motions?

6. Do you think Jesus ever disappointed people in his earthly ministry? Do you think Jesus knew this was inevitable?

7. Have you ever fallen victim to the myth of inadequate faith? How have you found it possible to move from re-

lying on your amount of faith to relying on the focus of your faith?

For Further Study

Beginner to Intermediate

Nouwen, Henri J. M. *The Return of the Prodigal: A Story of Homecoming.* New York: Doubleday, 1994.

Rolheiser, Ronald. *The Holy Longing: The Search for a Christian Spirituality.* New York: Doubleday Religion, 1999.

Wright, N. T. *Small Faith—Great God.* 2nd ed. Downers Grove, IL: InterVarsity Press, 2010.

More Advanced

Bird, Michael F., and Preston M. Sprinkle, eds. *The Faith of Jesus Christ: Exegetical, Biblical, and Theological Studies.* Milton Keynes, UK: Paternoster, 2009.

Mulholland Jr., M. Robert. *Invitation to a Journey: A Road Map for Spiritual Formation.* Downers Grove, IL: InterVarsity Press, 1993.

Smith, James K. A. *Desiring the Kingdom: Worship, Worldview, and Culture Formation.* Grand Rapids: Baker Academic, 2009.

5
GOD IS IN
CONTROL (?)

● ● ●

Lincoln's Log

Abraham Lincoln, in the wake of a calamitous defeat in
September 1862, scribbled down the following note, which has
since been named "Meditation on the Divine Will."

The will of God prevails. In great contests each party
claims to act in accordance with the will of God. Both may
be, and one must be, wrong. God cannot be for and against
the same thing at the same time. In the present civil war
it is quite possible that God's purpose is something different from the purpose of either party—and yet the human
instrumentalities, working just as they do, are of the best
adaptations to effect his purpose. I am almost ready to say
this is probably true—that God wills this contest, and wills
that it shall not end yet. By his mere great power, on the
minds of the now contestants, He could have either saved
or destroyed the Union without a human contest. Yet the

contest began. And, having begun He could give the final victory to either side any day. Yet the contest proceeds.[1]

Lincoln's words betray his deterministic understanding of a God who is fully in control of all things. Despite Lincoln's uncertainty of God's desires, his worldview allowed him to believe that the sovereign God sanctioned the Civil War. As Ronald C. White writes, "He was convinced that 'God wills this war,' but this conviction was balanced by his reluctance to equate God's will with the actions of either side."[2]

In 1865, Lincoln delivered his second inaugural address,[3] just a month before his assassination. Therein, he once again questioned whether God was for either side and asserted the possibility that God "gives to both North and South this terrible war as the woe due to those by whom the offense came."[4] The "offense," of course, was American slavery, and Lincoln described it as that "which, in the providence of God, must needs come, but which, having continued through His appointed time, He now wills to remove."[5]

In his former note, Lincoln seemed to rationalize the bloody conflict as an act of God's desires; in this inaugural address, he seemed to recognize it as an indictment on both sides. Lincoln's words seem contradictory. How can God punish humanity for a war God wills? How can slavery be both an offense of humanity and part of the providence of God? Lincoln's continued wrestling over the will of God was limited by his deterministic worldview. His belief in how God worked did not allow him to move past what he actually saw to be true— that humanity's sin was the cause of slavery and war, not God.

Instead, the lens of determinism clouded his vision, forming a log of irrational judgment (cf. Matt. 7:5).

This deterministic log is easily accessible in our world and in the church, and despite its long-term unreliability, it performs for us short-term results, which make it hard for us to see clearly what we should believe or to believe what we actually see.

Believing Is Seeing

We have all heard and possibly even used the maxim "seeing is believing." Rather than a statement of faith, it is usually understood as one of skepticism: *I will only believe it, if I see it.* Some have traced the origin of this phrase back to John 20:24-29 and the so-called story of doubting Thomas. However, the pejorative label *doubting* given to Thomas and the skeptical connotations surrounding the phrase *seeing is believing* may not be warranted.

Nowhere in the John narrative is the word *doubting* actually used, though some versions translate verse 27 this way (e.g., NIV reads "Stop doubting and believe"). What Jesus actually says is, "Do not be unbelieving, but believing" (NASB). Thomas is not devoid of faith; the last three years of his life prove this. Rather, he lacks the ability to understand a resurrected Messiah. The stress of the story is not on Thomas's skepticism but on Jesus's abundant grace, evidenced in his willingness to meet Thomas where he is and to help him move to a deeper level of faith.

Seeing before believing is actually a part of all the resurrection stories in chapter 20 of John's gospel. Peter and John do not believe Jesus's tomb is empty until they see for themselves, even after Mary tells them it is (v. 8). Jesus appears to Mary, and when she reports this to the disciples she exclaims, "I have seen the Lord" (v. 18). Jesus then appears to the disciples and shows them his hands and side, and we are told that "the disciples were overjoyed when they saw the Lord" (v. 20). In addition, when the disciples report this to Thomas, they exclaim, "We have seen the Lord" (v. 25). In other words, it appears that, often, seeing *is* believing.

But what are we to make of Jesus's closing statement to Thomas? "Because you have seen me, you have believed; blessed are those who have not seen and yet have believed" (v. 29). We must remember this is a gospel account, and as such, it is not primarily concerned with telling us a good story or with giving a historical account of Jesus's life. Its purpose is to move people to faith in Jesus as the risen Savior of the world. John knew people would need to read and hear these stories well after all the disciples and all those who had physically seen Jesus were gone. These accounts exist to provide physical proof in the absence of physical proof. Jesus's words are a reminder that his message will carry on and that his church will continue to grow and be blessed, all through a dynamic and growing faith in Christ.

We are, therefore, reminded that some people believe without seeing. In fact, believing usually leads *to* seeing. When we believe in someone or something, that belief leads to seeing the person or thing in a completely new way. Moreover, if the object of faith holds a position of high priority in a person's life, then this belief actually provides a lens by which much of reality is viewed, interpreted, and disseminated; it becomes a person's worldview, and this worldview can be both enlightening and blinding.

Dr. Jim Harries provides us with a perfect example of this reality in his study on the striking and often overlooked similarities between worldviews shaped by science and ones shaped by magic. He describes how both worldviews would interpret inconsistencies within the contexts of their default modes. For example, when people whose worldviews are shaped by science find new data that is outside of known metaphysical laws, they do not usually abandon their faith in science. They simply affirm that they are viewing data for which the scientific laws have "yet to be discovered."[6] Likewise, people with worldviews shaped by belief in magic do not automatically reject their faith when someone explains the scientific reason behind, for instance, why it rained. The science does not necessarily negate, for them, that there was still some magical power behind the event. Harries reminds us that "teaching someone in a way that appears contrary to their own deeply ingrained worldview may well not change their worldview, but simply extend its boundaries."[7] In other words, they will continue to see what they believe as opposed to believe what they see, no matter how strong the contrary evidence may be.

This paradoxical dual reality, that seeing can lead to believing, and believing can lead to seeing, means it is often difficult, though not impossible, to move people past their learned presumptions and premises. If we are truly responsible for what we know and what we do, then our challenge is to make sure our seeing is not clouded by wrong believing and that our believing is not distracted by a limited view of God, Scripture, or our world.

Learning to See

In chapter 9 of John's gospel, we find another interesting story as Jesus and his disciples encounter a man born blind. The disciples' question to Jesus is, "Rabbi, who sinned, this man or his parents, that he was born blind?" (v. 2). They are espousing the worldview of their day, that illness, deformity, and calamity are part of the judgment of God for human sin (think Job). Jesus's response would certainly take his pupils by surprise: "Neither this man nor his parents sinned" (v. 3). Yet the *New International Version*'s translation of Jesus's next line is even more disturbing than the disciples' question and the worldview that produces it. It reads, "but this happened so that the works of God might be displayed in him."[8] This translation makes it appear that God caused this man to be born blind, not because of anything the man or his parents did, but because God wanted to display his power by sending Jesus to heal the man many years later. This translation is not warranted, and moreover, it is theologically unfortunate.

Gary M. Burge, an expert on John's writings, has argued convincingly against the NIV translation. First, the words *this happened* are not present in the Greek. Second, the Greek purpose clause translated "so that" can grammatically be connected to what follows, just as easily as it could be connected to what precedes. Burge's translation therefore connects verses 3 and 4 and reads: "'Neither this man nor his parents sinned,' said Jesus. 'But so that the work of God might be displayed in his life, we must do the work of him who sent me while it is still day.'"[9] The difference is theologically enormous, "God had not made the man blind in order to show his glory; rather, God has sent Jesus to do works of healing in order to show his glory."[10]

In other words, Jesus's response extends the conversation beyond an issue of blame, to an issue of responsibility and participation, how God wants to work through us to bring about restoration and justice. Jesus invites the disciples to be part of the solution, not just for this young man, but for overcoming the erroneous worldview in which God is ultimately to be blamed for everything that happens.

The whole narrative speaks to the dual themes of responsibility and overcoming erroneous worldviews. For instance, the miracle itself is somewhat unique. Instead of merely healing the man, Jesus puts mud on his eyes, then tells him to go wash off the mud in the Pool of Siloam. It is only after the man follows through with this task that he can see (v. 7). What would you have done? Many would have walked away, thinking Jesus was crazy. He did just make mud from his own spit and rub it on the man's eyes. Furthermore, it could not have been easy for a blind man to find his way to this pool; he likely would have had to ask someone for help, which would have been more embarrassing than normal, since his face was covered in mud. Just like the disciples, this man needed to learn how to see anew, and this took time and responsibility.

As the narrative develops, the juxtaposition of the religious leaders and the healed man proves ironic. Those who have physically seen for their whole lives are spiritually and even physically unable to see what is right in front of them, while the man born blind is now able to see both physically *and* spiritually. For these Pharisees, Jesus is a sinner because he heals on the Sabbath (v. 16). In their thinking this means either the miracle is not from God (v. 29), or this man was never really blind and, thus, not really healed (v. 18). Even after the man and his parents confirm that he was born blind, the Pharisees hold on to doubt. They cannot see past their preconceived judgments, though all the evidence points toward an alternate truth; their beliefs prevent them from seeing. The narrative even recounts that the healed man is so astonished at their unbelief that he logically and ironically, like a trained rabbi, walks them through the facts as he understands them (vv. 30-33). To which the Pharisees reply, "You were steeped in sin at birth; how dare you lecture us" (v. 34). When all else fails, they return to the safety of their erroneous worldview.

Jesus attempts to shift the disciples' worldview and broaden their scope of vision so they can see the tragedies of their world from a different perspective. He is calling us to this same shift. Like the religious leaders in this story, we are too often crippled by our biased judgments. We see people living on the streets and think of the paltry number of reasons we can imagine why they might be there. We see a young mother in a supermarket using food stamps and assume she is playing the system. We hear about a teenager shot in a less-than-reputable neighborhood and immediately jump to conclusions about the activities in which that teenager was likely involved.

Like the healed man, like the disciples, we need to learn to see anew. Jesus invites us to participate in actively shifting a dominant Christian worldview that has done more to place God on the judgment seat than to show God's love. Jesus has invited us to take responsibility by asking ourselves how God wants to work through us to bring about restoration and justice in each and every situation we encounter.

God Is in Control

The question of whether God is in control does not have a clear-cut, yes-or-no answer. It really depends on what people mean when they utter these words. If one means God is the cause of all events, both good and bad, then our answer is an adamant no! Nor do we accept the idea that God controls humanity's choices, making us mindless robots. However, if by "God is in control" one means that God is the ultimate Creator, Sustainer, and Redeemer of all things, then we can absolutely say yes.

God as Creator, Sustainer, and Redeemer is part of the relational nature of who God is. God's love prevents God from walking away from that which he has created, and even moves God toward redeeming that which humanity has tried to destroy. Have no doubts about it: God is moving all things toward restoration and re-creation, but he is not doing it through manipulation or magic; he is doing it through love! This is what differentiates him from the passive god of deism and the controlling god of determinism.

We tend to define *control* as "restraint" or "dominance." We think of it as the wielding of power, but God thinks of it as the yielding of power. In other words, God shows his power by releasing and distributing it. God exemplifies control in terms of presence and freedom. We have already spoken about how this self-yielding is seen in God's creating humanity with free will; it is then seen, following the fall, in giving free grace through the cross of Christ, where such self-yielding is vividly displayed. To this, we add that it is also clearly seen through the giving of the Holy Spirit.

The Holy Spirit is given as a constant companion to the believer. In John 14–16, Jesus refers to the Holy Spirit as *paraclētos*, meaning "one who is called beside," and is thus correctly translated as "helper," "advocate," "counselor," or "comforter." This God-presence indwells, empowers, teaches, guides, even convicts—but never manipulates. As the apostle Paul reminds us, it is through the Holy Spirit that "God's love has been poured out into our hearts" (Rom. 5:5). Furthermore, in Romans 8—the richest and longest statement about the role of the Holy Spirit—we learn, among other things, that the Spirit "gives life" and helps free us "from the law of sin and death" (vv. 2, 10), helps us put to death the "misdeeds" of the flesh (v. 13), and cries out to God in our weakness (vv. 26-27). As Klyne Snodgrass puts it, "The Spirit is the power of God at work in people."[11]

God the Father, through Jesus's life, death, and resurrection, and through the Holy Spirit's presence, is not controlling us but freeing us. In fact, God's love is so strong that God constantly seeks to free us from anything that might dominate or control us, even that which we brought upon ourselves, such as sin and death. He even wants to free us from our constrictive and erroneous worldviews. God does not accumulate power but disseminates it and, in so doing, reveals to us the true nature of control. God is so big and so self-sustaining that God does not need our affirmation, our worship, or our feeble power. Instead, God invites us to embrace God's power and live out of it. God invites us to join him in loving rather than manipulating, in serving rather than being served, and in yielding power rather than wielding it.

None of this takes away from who God is or what God is able to do. It just shows us that God is "able to do immeasurably more than all we ask or imagine, according to his power that is at work within us" (Eph. 3:20). The paradox is that God does these things through love and influence rather than through power and manipulation. This is why it is "immeasurably more than all we ask or imagine." If God did it the way we asked and the way we imagined, it would, at best, involve taking away someone else's rights to help ourselves or someone we loved, and at worst, it would involve greed, power, manipulation, violence, and war. These are the things humans do best. They are what we understand. As hard as we try to fight against these tendencies, if left to our own limited understanding and imaginations, we will inevitably fail. This is why God does not do it our way, and this is why it is so difficult for us to comprehend. It is counterintuitive to our fallen nature.

Even more paradoxical than God's way of unmanipulated control is that the Ephesians passage speaks of God's power being "at work within us." This is clearly connected to the preceding prayer by Paul:

> I pray that out of his glorious riches he may strengthen you with power through his Spirit in your inner being, so that Christ may dwell in your hearts through faith. And I pray that you, being rooted and established in love, may have power, together with all the Lord's holy people, to grasp how wide and long and high and deep is the love of Christ, and to know this love that surpasses knowledge—that you

may be filled to the measure of all the fullness of God. (Eph. 3:16-19)

God desires, through the Holy Spirit, to work his power within us. Not the manipulative power of the world, but the loving power of the cross. If we will let it, this loving power will grow in us until it shatters the limits of our human knowledge and thinking and fills us so full we overflow into the world. To be clear, this is not an individual process; every *you* and *your* in this passage is plural for a reason. True growth in God's love takes place together as we are rooted in God. This does not mean it is not personal; relationship is always personal. But it does mean it is primarily corporate. This prayer is about God's power and authority at work in God's church. We are that church, and God's power and authority are at work in us so that it may be at work through us. Paul's prayer for the church is a prayer of love for the world.

Greater Things than These

This new picture of God's control through presence and freedom, God's yielding of power, and God's love manifested in and through God's responsible people coalesces in these words:

Very truly I tell you, whoever believes in me will do the works I have been doing, and they will do even greater things than these, because I am going to the Father. (John 14:12)

Our first reaction is no doubt to shake our heads and ask, "What was God thinking?" Why would God trust us with such an important task? Bruce Epperly suggests many have difficulty understanding this opportunity because they view the world through a "zero sum" lens, which sees all of life as a competition where there can be only one winner. Therefore, God either has to be completely sovereign or completely impotent, completely controlling or completely passive. Epperly suggests that in this traditional scarcity model of human and divine agency, any creativity or initiative by humans must be viewed as a threat on the divine, a potential act of disobedience. Any person, persons, or institutions that appear to usurp God's power are accused of playing God.[12]

Those holding this worldview are forced by their limited picture of God toward self-defense, fearing their God might actually be destroyed. Passages such as John 14:12 are seen as an affront because they suggest a partnership between God and humanity that threatens God's sovereignty and control. Yet this is only a threat for those holding to a theology of certainty. If God's control is actually a yielding of power through presence and freedom, then John 14:12 makes perfect sense. As Epperly writes:

> Creaturely freedom does not challenge divine creativity but enables God to do new and creative things. The more healthy and creative freedom creatures embody in their actions, the greater freedom and power God can embody in God's ongoing activity in the world.[13]

Wow! This is such a dynamic collaboration it is almost unfathomable. But it should not be. This is the nature of divine love. Love is expansive! It must reach out, and it must reproduce. For many, this picture of love as expansive is foreign. They are so afraid of losing love that when they actually find it, they smother it to death. God does the opposite. God gives love away freely, and since God is love, this means God gives himself away. John 14 is all about this. Jesus is about to give his life away on the cross, but first he needs to give the disciples the assurance of his presence through the Holy Spirit. And, with this assurance, he passes the torch to his disciples. Jesus frees them to continue his mission. He frees *us* for mission! We are an extension of his love in the world.

Yes, God would do a better job than we would. Yes, God knew we would falter and even fail at points. Yes, this was a risk for God.

Most of our *why* questions arise out of our worldly need to manipulate and control each and every situation. We think that by doing this, we can guarantee stability and success. This, however, is not God's aim. God does not wish to control the situation through manipulation but, rather, in love, to release us with God's presence so we might freely return this love to God through others.

Even though we are obviously free to make wrong choices, God's desire, God's expectation, is that we will be transformed by his ever-present love. In other words, God's love wants to expand in us as well. God knows our potential, and God actually does expect us to take responsibility for who we are, who we are becoming, and even for the world around us. This is why God says, "If you love me, keep my commands" (John 14:15). This is not a command, certainly not an ultimatum. It is an invitation to genuine relationship. It is an invitation to live out of God's authority and to live God's kind of authority in the world. It is an invitation to do what God has done. It is even an invitation to do greater things than God has done!

Questions for Further Reflection or Small Group Discussion

1. Which do you think typically comes first, seeing or believing?
2. React to this statement: "When we believe in someone or something, that belief leads to seeing the person or thing in a completely new way."
3. When was the last time you felt difficulty moving someone past his or her learned presumptions? When was the last time you had trouble moving past your own learned presumptions?
4. Do you think past leaders such as Abraham Lincoln were limited because of the presumptions of their deterministic worldviews? Why or why not?
5. What assumptions did you notice that you have made about people this past week? Which of these judgments do you think were accurate? Which do you think were false?
6. How do you define control? How do you define what it means for God to be in control?
7. React to this statement: "God knows our potential, and God actually does expect us to take responsibility."

For Further Study

Beginner to Intermediate

Burge, Gary M. *John*. The NIV Application Commentary. Grand Rapids: Zondervan, 2000.

Giberson, Karl. *Worlds Apart: The Unholy War between Religion and Science*. Kansas City: Beacon Hill Press of Kansas City, 1993.

Middleton, J. Richard, and Brian J. Walsh. *Truth Is Stranger Than It Used to Be: Biblical Faith in a Postmodern Age*. Downers Grove, IL: InterVarsity Press, 1995.

More Advanced

Hays, Richard B. *The Moral Vision of the New Testament: A Contemporary Introduction to New Testament Ethics*. New York: HarperCollins, 1996.

McIntosh, Mark. *Mysteries of Faith*. The New Church's Teaching Series, vol. 8. Lanham, MD: Cowley Publications, 2000.

Wright, Christopher J. H. *The Mission of God: Unlocking the Bible's Grand Narrative*. Downers Grove, IL: InterVarsity Press, 2006.

6
UNSOLVED MYSTERIES

• • •

Participating in the Mystery

Created by Sir Arthur Conan Doyle, Sherlock Holmes is a well-known fictional detective who, along with Dr. Watson, has captivated hearts and imaginations for more than a century. The past few years have seen a resurgence of this dynamic duo in films, on television, and in a new book.[1]

What is it about Sherlock Holmes that is so captivating? Could it be that we see Holmes as a kind of relatable superhero? As opposed to the magical superheroes we are used to, Holmes is mysterious, but his powers do not go beyond the realm of possibility. He amazes us with his masterful disguises, astute observations, insightful logic, and forensic skills. Holmes is a believable superhero, a superhero for the information age, an age where everything is accessible.

A great example of Holmes's superhero-like abilities is witnessed in his first encounter with Watson, in the novel *A Study in Scarlet.*[2] A common friend named Mike Stamford introduces them but does not offer any background information. Instead, Holmes deduces everything he needs to know about the former army doctor simply by observing him for a few brief moments. At first glance, Holmes appears to possess some type of magical ability of observation, but Holmes is not magical; quite the opposite. Holmes is mysterious, and he invites Watson and others to join him in the mystery.

In the novel *The Hound of the Baskervilles*, Holmes sends Watson to do a bit of observational investigation. Later, in a late-night encounter, Watson discovers that Holmes has been present, and working secretly, all along. Watson's first reaction is relief as he states, "Indeed the responsibility and the mystery were both becoming too much for my nerves."[3] Then his mood swings toward bitterness as he wonders whether Holmes's presence is a sign of distrust and whether all his work has been in vain. After much dialogue, Holmes is able to convince Watson that he and his work are invaluable and that the ruse was necessary. Watson expresses the realization that he played a vital role in the midst of this mystery and that his participation was a necessary part of the process.

This willingness for Holmes to allow Watson the freedom to engage the mystery himself is a great illustration of the journey in which God invites us to participate. Herein lies the difference between magic and mystery. Magic leaves us in awe, but we walk away unchanged. When we think about magic, we think of the superheroes who do what we could never do. Therefore, we forfeit control, freedom, even responsibility, to allow them to do their work. In magic, we are left powerless, waiting for Superman.

Mystery is different. It invites us to participate. Likewise, God is not magical; God is mysterious, and God invites us to participate in him and in his grand mystery. And as we do, we ourselves begin to learn more about God and about the world around us. We begin to see *what* God sees and even begin to see *as* God sees.

Reimagining Authority

A myth exists in modern society that those who believe in God are naïve and weak, that they need a crutch; whereas, those who are atheistic (or at least deistic) are free to be themselves, not dominated or coerced by God. Is this really the case? Or could it be that those who view themselves as independent are really just trapped under the authority of gods of which they are unaware or unwilling to name? Richard Dawkins and other secular humanists justifiably attack the faith of those who comply with visions of a God that are manipulative and dictatorial. However, even they must admit that no one is ever free in the sense of being uninfluenced. So which is preferable, the gods of consumerism, materialism, entertainment, and power, or the Christian God? Sadly, for many Christians, these are one and the same.

Michael Reeves has suggested that God might have some public relations work to do. He wonders if the obvious hostility toward God by many is actually a rejection of God or only a rejection of a certain type of god—a god they believe is a loveless dictator in the sky. Could it be that this type of anti-theism is really an "unknowing hunger for a better God"?[4] This "better God" is the one we have been trying to reveal through this book. He is not the God of control or the God of passivity, but the God of relationship. He is interested in conversation and participation. He is the triune God—Father, Son, and Holy Spirit—working together to transform this world through love and not through magic and manipulation.

If God is not a god of magic, dominating and determining every measure of our lives, then how do we relate to God? Ronald Heifetz, in his work *Leadership without Easy Answers*, describes a new vision for how leadership and the role of authority fit in to our modern society. Maybe his work can help us reimagine our relationship to God's authority and even God's relationship to our authority.

Heifetz begins his work on authority by affirming that all social relationships have to understand how authority works. To ignore this would be like a plane manufacturer ignoring gravity.[5] For example, Heifetz describes how, within communities of chimpanzees and gorillas, the dominant members help control several social functions. These include directing group movement, protecting from predators, orienting members toward status and place, controlling conflict, and maintaining norms.[6]

Certainly traditional views of God's activity could be equated with these, and no doubt, these issues relate to our sense of divine providence. Christians have often found comfort in a worldview where someone must control these things for us. The persons we think offer this kind of control are the people we normally equate with magic (whether we are conscious of it or not); they are the untouchable superheroes who move us toward complacency. Throughout history, people have traditionally related to God using words such as *sovereign* and *almighty*, and these are certainly indisputable attributes of God. Nevertheless, if we transition to a theology of luck, we must reevaluate how we view our relationship to the Almighty.

Heifetz argues that just because dominance and hierarchy seem to succeed in providing stability in animal societies, this is not proof of their importance and necessity in all of created order. Just because someone *does* dominate does not mean that person *should* dominate. Heifetz defines true authority as "conferred power to perform a service,"[7] stating that while "dominance relationships are based on coercion or habitual deference; authority relationships are voluntary and conscious."[8] Relationships based in dominance—or magic—must be seen as coercion or manipulation. Instead, Heifetz argues for leading through authority that is conferred on someone as a mutual exchange.

To illustrate the movement from deferment to conferment, Heifetz uses the relationship between parents and children. Children defer to their parents often without thought. They are desperate and in need, incapable of making decisions or providing for themselves otherwise. However, over time, children develop the ability to make their own decisions and to provide for their own needs. Thus, the child-parent relationship must change as children begin to realize their parents' desire for them to share in the responsibility. Here is where authority becomes a mutual exchange. Just as the parents must now confer authority on the child, the newly developing adolescent must choose to confer authority back on the parent; it can no longer be given through acquiescence or taken by coercion.

However, for a number of reasons, two of which stand out, this transition from deferment to conferment does not always take place. First, from the standpoint of the dominant party, surrender of authority is not always easy since it means a loss of control. Second, from the standpoint of the dominated party, deferring to an authority can yield certain payoffs, including a sense of stability, a neglect of responsibility, and someone to blame when things go wrong.

Christians have blindly deferred authority to God for far too long. Some do this because of an erroneous belief that God desires this action from his creation. Others do this because they enjoy the payoffs. Either way, blind deferment is not a relationship, and we must find a way to move past it and embrace the dynamic God who has conferred authority on his people through a yielding of power. True worship of this God means conferring authority back on God. Not through acquiescence or manipulation but through participation. God's conferment of authority upon us is a gift. It is a vote of confidence in us. We cannot allow this gift to remain unwrapped and unused or to be thrown aside. Instead, we must embrace the authority within, which is given through the indwelling Holy Spirit, and live it out. A theology of luck calls for people to share in the mysterious movement of God's desires in the world.

Participating in God

The concept of "God in us" is hard to grasp, though we must (e.g., Rom. 8:9-11; Gal. 2:20; Col. 1:26-27). But the concept of "us in God" is almost unfathomable. Nevertheless, God does not just invite us to be in relationship; God invites us to be in him by being in Christ, through the Spirit. In the paraphrased words of John 15:4, God's invitation is to

> live in me. Make your home in me just as I do in you. In the same way that a branch can't bear grapes by itself but only by being joined to the vine, you can't bear fruit unless you are joined with me. (MSG)

God calls us to inhabit him—to be so intimately connected that our lives bear God's fruit.

In the same way, the apostle Paul speaks of this participation in Christ and with Christ so often[9] that many see it as the central tenet of his theology.[10] Perhaps the clearest picture of this comes in 1 Corinthians 6:15-17, where Paul speaks about the mysterious union between us and God to illustrate why those in Corinth should stay clear of sexual impurities:

> Do you not know that your bodies are members of Christ himself? Shall I then take the members of Christ and unite them with a prostitute? Never! Do you not know that he who unites himself with a prostitute is one with her in body? For it is said, "The two will become one flesh." But whoever is united with the Lord is one with him in spirit.

Paul uses the marriage metaphor from Genesis 2:24 to speak of the intimate connection that takes place between believers and God. Somehow, we become one. This is not a sterile union; it is not about saying "I do" and then continuing to live separate lives. This is a real marriage, where we are invited to grow deeper in relationship with God daily. Lest we take this metaphor too far, Paul is not saying that we *become* God or that we have somehow been consumed into the Godhead. Rather, by participating in God, we become *like* God more and more each day. We begin to take on God's nature, which means taking on God's love, which means taking on God's mission.

This union and participation in God are simultaneously union and participation in the body of Christ, the church. In fact, in Paul, these two ideas are inseparable. Christ is the Head; we are the body. There is an amazing and mysterious synergy that takes place as we become one with Christ. Just as the Father, Son, and Holy Spirit—though separate beings—share in a common substance, so we, too, though separate persons, share in a common substance (the Holy Spirit) with one another and with the Godhead. "So in Christ we, though many, form one body, and each member belongs to all the others" (Rom. 12:5). We each remain unique with unique gifts, but we all use these gifts for the same purpose. We are called together to live out the Great Commandment (Matt. 22:38-40) and the Great Commission (28:19-20). This is clearly reflected in Jesus's prayer to the Father:

> Father, just as you are in me and I am in you. May they also be in us so that the world may believe that you have sent me. I have given them the glory that you gave me, that they may be one as we are one—I in them and you in me—so that they may be brought to complete unity. Then the world will know that you sent me and have loved them even as you have loved me. (John 17:21*b*-23)

There is something mysterious about this union that takes place (or should take place), which makes the world around us stand up and take notice. Like a giant puzzle, when Christians come together as one under one Head, the world gets an incredible picture of God; it may be a montage of unique faces, but the only thing other people see is the extent of God's love.

Participating in God does not just change the way the world sees us; it changes the way we see the world, the way we see reality, because Christ's life, death, and resurrection inaugurated a new age, the eschatological age. *Eschatology* is a fancy word that is used by many to talk about the end times. However, the word is better translated "a study of last things" and concerns anything that is connected to God's consummation of all things. In order to unpack this complex phenomenon we must start by looking at some background information.

Throughout the Old Testament there are significant signposts pointing to a new age when . . .

God would raise up a Messiah to establish his kingdom:

The LORD declares to you that the LORD himself will establish a house for you: When your days are over and you rest with your ancestors, I will raise up your offspring to succeed you, your own flesh and blood, and I will establish his kingdom. He is the one who will build a house for my Name, and I will establish the throne of his kingdom forever. I will be his father, and he will be my son. (2 Sam. 7:11-14*a*)

God would write his law in our hearts:

"This is the covenant I will make with the people of Israel
    after that time," declares the LORD.
"I will put my law in their minds
    and write it on their hearts.
I will be their God,

and they will be my people." (Jer. 31:33)

God would give his people his Spirit:

And afterward,

> I will pour out my Spirit on all people.

Your sons and daughters will prophesy,

> your old men will dream dreams,

> your young men will see visions.

Even on my servants, both men and women,

> I will pour out my Spirit in those days.

I will show wonders in the heavens

> and on the earth,

> blood and fire and billows of smoke. (Joel 2:28-30)

God would create "new heavens and a new earth":

See, I will create

> new heavens and a new earth.

The former things will not be remembered,

> nor will they come to mind.

But be glad and rejoice forever

> in what I will create,

for I will create Jerusalem to be a delight

> and its people a joy.

I will rejoice over Jerusalem

> and take delight in my people;

the sound of weeping and of crying

> will be heard in it no more. (Isa. 65:17-19)

This age is known by many names: day of the Lord, age of the Spirit, messianic age, kingdom of God/heaven, and the age to come. The Israelites wait with expectation and certainty for God to fulfill the promises given through his prophets and in his Word. The New Testament reveals that this long-awaited age has indeed come in the person and work of Christ, yet it has not come in its fullness. Yes, the Messiah has come; yes, the Holy Spirit has been given; yes, God's kingdom reign has begun; but these things are signs pointing to the consummation of the age when the new heaven and new earth will become a reality and God's rule will be acknowledged by all (see Rev. 21:1-5).

Here is where things get a bit confusing. The Israelite people understand that all of these phenomena will take place simultaneously. They believe that on the day of the Lord, the Messiah will come and bring salvation to the righteous, judgment to the unrighteous, and restoration to all creation. They believe that God's Spirit will be poured out and God's kingdom fully established, all in a single event. So when they do not see all these things taking place, many doubt whether Christ is truly the long-awaited Messiah (remember the stories of Peter and John the Baptist) and whether the new age has actually begun.

But God does not do it the way everyone expects him to do it. Instead, this new age is inaugurated through Christ's first coming and awaits its fulfillment in Christ's second coming. We, therefore, live between these two ages. We live in the time between the times, between the "already" and the "not yet." God postpones the fulfillment of these things for the sake of grace and love. This interim period is a time for people to discover the depths of the Father's love, exemplified in the Son, made known through the Holy Spirit, and (expected to be) lived out by the church.

Those who are in Christ are already part of this new reality. In the words of the apostle Paul: "Therefore, if anyone is in Christ, the new creation has come: The old has gone, the new is here" (2 Cor. 5:17). Though this passage has often been erroneously individualized, it is not primarily about becoming new creations. Rather, it is about joining God's already-not-yet new creation. We are those who have recognized the reign of the King and willingly submitted to his authority. We are, therefore, already kingdom people, already living in the age to come, already experiencing the Spirit's work in our lives and in our world, already seeing the justice of God at work through God's people.

The certainty of the future has broken into the present, and we call it hope. This hope is not given for our comfort, though it does bring comfort. It is not given so we can sit back and do nothing. Rather, this hope transforms us and moves us to action. Like love, hope is expansive in the present. As we reside in Christ and, thus, in this new age, we are indeed changed and made new, but more than that, and more importantly, we are people who help to make all things new. We have been tasked with the great responsibility and the great authority to reveal the already-not-yet kingdom to the world around us. This is indeed a great mystery, and we are part of the unveiling of it, helping to make it less mysterious to the world around us.

A Holy Vocation

It is indeed a mystery that God would choose to use a small group of people to reveal God's kingdom and love to the rest of humanity. Yet we should not be surprised since from Abraham to Moses, from Deborah to Ruth, from David to Elijah, and on and on, the Scriptures reveal this same strategy.

Think of the disciples for a moment. Jesus's earthly ministry lasts only three years, and in that time Jesus does not organize a business or develop a marketing plan to reach the masses. Instead, he invests the majority of his time in twelve disciples. Moreover, these twelve are not exactly the cream of the crop. They are average, some even below average. They are not the smartest, the most honest, or the bravest. Yet Jesus chooses this motley crew to be his missionary plan to reach the world—because Jesus is relational!

Relationships are not developed by organizations, business plans, websites, billboards, or even buildings. Relationships occur when one person intentionally invests time, energy, and love into another person. It happens on the small scale rather than on the large scale. Try as we have, we just cannot shortcut authentic relationships. God's desire is that these twelve pour their lives into others and that those others then pour their lives into still more people. One relationship at a time, God is revealed, God's love is shared, and the church grows.

This is a work of love, and each of us has been called to this joint holy vocation. We are a royal priesthood who have been called out of darkness to declare the praises of the one who called us (1 Pet. 2:9-10). We must remember, however, that this is not done in our own strength but in participation with God. It is a joint venture of love. In the words of Miroslav Volf:

> God does not call a person to do anything for which God does not give her the ability. It is not, therefore, her duty to do whatever morally acceptable work the situation in which

she lives might demand of her. It is her privilege to do the kind of work for which God's Spirit has gifted her.[11]

This work is not easy, especially at first. Relationships are messy, and some of those whom Christ has called us to love will inevitably lash out against us. Jesus's death is proof of this. However, like Jesus, we must approach our vocation with motivation and determination. Jesus does not enter into the journey of the cross because he desires pain or glory but because he loves the Father and his creation.

In the same way, we must be motivated by God's love. This means we cannot seek to manipulate or coerce people to faith. We cannot love them for the sole purpose of saving their souls. We cannot love them only when it is convenient. We cannot offer relationship then take it away when they do something that bothers or hurts us. We must be sacrificial in our love because it is not ours to withhold, just as it is not ours to give. It is God's love working through us, and God's love is always sacrificial.

Jesus's prayer at Gethsemane (Mark 14:35-36) reminds us that even when we know the difficult path ahead of us, when the moment is upon us, when the pain is so near and real we can taste its bitterness, we will likely attempt to avoid it at all costs. "Take this cup from me" (v. 36) will probably be a common plea among us. But, like Jesus, we, too, must complete the prayer: "Yet not what I will, but what you will" (v. 36). Jesus does not defer to God's will because he has to but because he trusts that the Father's desires are worth leaning into. Likewise, we will not be forced down the path of this holy vocation, at least not by God. We have a choice. Many times along the way we will choose selfishness, choose safety, choose to avoid pain. But those choices will only lead to greater pain, for us and for our world.

God has invited us into this marvelous and mysterious journey where we partner with God to bring love and change to the world. It is scary, not because we do not know what will happen or where God might lead us (this may or may not be the case); it is scary because it means letting go of control as we know it and embracing the depths of God's ever expansive love. In the words of Catherine Keller:

> Embracing the depths of life, in which are mingled the depths of divinity itself, we participate in an open-ended creativity. We no longer huddle within the frozen order of an absolute power, waiting to be saved from the creation itself. We are called into a process of interaction with our fellow creatures—and with the one who calls us forth.[12]

Questions for Further Reflection or Small Group Discussion

1. Have you noticed the resurgence of the character of Sherlock Holmes? What do you think is so captivating about Doyle's character?

2. What is the difference between magic and mystery as described in this chapter? Do you agree or disagree?

3. Do you agree that people who may reject certain visions of God also unknowingly hunger for a "better God"?

4. Have you ever felt comfort in the traditional idea that God controls everything? Do you think this idea is a healthy vision of reality?

5. What is the difference between deferring to authority and conferring authority as regards an authority like God?

6. What do you think it means to be *in Christ*?

7. React to this thought: "As we reside in Christ . . . we are indeed changed and made new, but more than that, and more importantly, we are people who help to make all things new."

For Further Study

Beginner to Intermediate

Brueggemann, Walter. *Awed to Heaven, Rooted in Earth: Prayers of Walter Brueggemann.* Minneapolis: Fortress Press, 2003.

Reeves, Michael. *Delighting in the Trinity: An Introduction to the Christian Faith.* Downers Grove, IL: InterVarsity Press, 2012.

Stewart, James S. *A Man in Christ: The Vital Elements of St. Paul's Religion.* New York: Harper and Row, 1935.

More Advanced

Boyer, Steven D., and Christopher A. Hall. *The Mystery of God: Theology for Knowing the Unknowable.* Grand Rapids: Baker Academic, 2012.

Campbell, Constantine R. *Paul and Union with Christ: An Exegetical and Theological Study.* Grand Rapids: Zondervan, 2012.

Volf, Miroslav. *Work in the Spirit: Toward a Theology of Work.* Eugene, OR: Wipf and Stock, 2001.

THE MOVEMENT FROM DESTINY TO DESIRE

○ ○ ○

What is our response to this God?

What is our responsibility in this world?

7
GOD'S ACTIVITY

• • •

Soul Mates?

Although the first usage of the term *soul mate* did not appear in the English language until 1822,[1] it has a long prior history. The great philosopher Plato (ca. 428–348 BC), in his work *Symposium*, recounts the Greek playwright Aristophanes's (448–385 BC) mythological story of the origins of humanity and love. Aristophanes tells of how humans were once androgynous, being both male and female, with two faces, four arms and legs, and so on. However, they were so powerful that they threatened the gods, so Zeus cut them in half, forming two separate beings. Therefore, these two halves yearn for one another as they seek to be reunited.

And when one of them meets with his other half, the actual half of himself . . . the pair are lost in an amazement of love and friendship and intimacy, and would not be out of the other's sight, as I may say, even for a moment: these are the people who pass their whole lives together; yet they could not explain what they desire of one another. For the intense yearning which each of them has towards the other does not appear to be the desire of lover's intercourse, but of something else which the soul of either evidently desires and cannot tell, and of which she has only a dark and doubtful presentiment.[2]

Similarly, the Jewish mystical work known as the *Zohar* recounts how twin souls, composed of both male and female, are split and sent out, "predestined before birth to reunite in matrimony."[3] In this way they are meant to be together. These two long-lost souls reunite on earth and complete the perfection that God created them for, according to God's desires.

These concepts have been perpetuated down to the modern era, and the general idea that there is one perfect person out there for everyone is held by many today. Likewise, many Christians hold a similar view and often equate it with the concept of God's divine will. This idea makes sense for those who believe God has determined all things. If God has predestined the small things, then of course he has predestined the large things. Right? Take, for example, Janet (Folger) Porter, a popular Christian radio personality, writer, and activist. Though she is now married, she has been outspoken on many of her views, including her perspective on singleness. Here are a few lines from an interview with the Christian Broadcasting Network, before she was married:

> I think that there is one that He wants for you. I think that we can mess up. People divorce. God hates divorce. People do it all of the time. But I believe that if we are surrendered to Him and we are submitted to Him and we are seeking Him first, then these things are going to be added. It is go-

ing to be the person that He has. We can marry Mr. Will Do or Mr. Good Enough, and He can make good from that, but I don't think it is His best. I want His best, and I honestly think He has a best. If He has every day planned, He knows who that is.[4]

There are several things wrong with Porter's theological picture. For instance, those who "mess up" and marry the wrong person have no choice but to settle, since "God hates divorce." If followed to its logical conclusion, this would mean that each person who marries the so-called wrong person actually deprives two other people of marrying the right person. After all, if there is a perfect, chosen person for everyone, and Person 1 and Person 2 chose wrong, then Person 3 (whom Person 1 was supposed to marry) and Person 4 (whom Person 2 was supposed to marry) will be forced to settle for Person 5 and Person 6. We now have a minimum of six people in wrong relationships, with at least another two (those who were supposed to marry Persons 5 and 6) out of luck. It does not take a mathematician to tell you that, before long, it becomes mathematically impossible for anyone to marry the one, single, individual person God ordained for him or her.

Another problem with Porter's view, and other views like it, is that it gives many people an excuse to give up on their marriages. They either divorce in search of their soul mates or physically and emotionally check out of their marriages while remaining in them legally. They are left hopeless. After all, if their spouses are not the ones they were supposed to be with, then no matter what they do, they will never be truly happy.

These two often conflated concepts of *soul mate* and *God's will* do not actually speak of love; they speak of destiny.

Along for the Ride or on the Hunt

Destiny, like fate, is equated with inevitability. People tend to associate destiny with positive outcomes and fate with negative outcomes, but they are basically synonymous; and from the perspective of this book, they are both negative because those whose lives are dictated by these phenomena are either along for the ride or on the hunt. They either relinquish power and responsibility as they wait for their fate to unfold, or they aggressively search out their destiny regardless of who or what they destroy along the way.

Of course, destiny and fate are rarely tied to trivial matters. One does not say, "It was my destiny to eat a ham sandwich today," or "I was fated to have my cavity filled today." Instead, it is usually connected to the most significant life decisions, things such as marriage, family, and career. The aforementioned soulmates illustration speaks to the importance of relationships and of love in our world. Relationships serve as an example of how believing in the concept of destiny shapes our actions toward a philosophy of either *along for the ride* or *on the hunt*.

The song "Bless the Broken Road,"[5] which was popularized by Rascal Flatts, highlights the *on the hunt* attitude of destiny and incriminates God along the way. Some of the key lines are:

I couldn't see how every sign pointed straight to you

·   ·   ·

Others who broke my heart they were like northern stars
Pointing me on my way into your loving arms

•   -   •

. . . God blessed the broken road
That led me straight to you

•   -   •

It's all part of a grander plan that is coming true[6]

This song perpetuates the romantic idea that, despite distance and difficulty, eventually we find our soul mate. We may need to struggle down the path and through various wrong relationships until we find our destiny, but God will bless our efforts. Can you see the problems with this picture of God? This God sends us on scavenger hunts through pain and brokenness to find a prize. Those lucky enough to find the prize look back on the difficult path, say it was all worth it, and even thank God for the journey. However, those left alone and broken on the road often feel cursed by God. Furthermore, many go from relationship to relationship, waiting for some magic feeling or some audible word from God to validate the relationship. Opportunities for love are lost when people spend their time searching for "the one," and many people get hurt along the way.

The other side of the destiny coin is those people who embrace the attitude of *along for the ride.* Instead of hunting down their destiny, they sit back and wait for their destiny to find them. As an example, many are no doubt familiar with the Anglican theologian and churchman John Stott, who was known for his public theology but also for his personal celibacy. Stott was open about his singleness and its relationship to not having a sense of the certainty of God's will in this area of his life. He admitted that while he never made a vow of celibacy, he did attempt to remain single until God moved him to action. In his youth, he thought he would one day marry, but he never found a woman whom he believed was God's choice for his life partner, so he began to believe God meant him to remain single. Looking back, he said, "I think I know why. I could never have traveled or written as extensively as I have done if I had had the responsibilities of a wife and family."[7]

While this last point is probably true, we are not sold on the idea that God did not want him to get married just because he did not sense some assurance from God. In fact, it appears he did not sense this assurance in either direction. We have nothing against singleness, or against marriage, for that matter. Furthermore, we do not know all the details of Stott's situation and so do not want to make firm judgments about it. Yet it is interesting that many find themselves in a similar situation as they wait for love. They wait for a yes from God before they act. Why not wait for a no from God before they stop? One starts with action; the other, inaction.

God's Word does not give a general command not to enter a relationship until he gives the okay. It does, however, speak of the expansiveness of love and evidences a desire for humanity to live out the often difficult task of loving those around us. Often, in this active loving, we will find someone with whom we have a deep connection and about whom we believe it is worth investing the time and energy needed to make the relationship (any relationship) a success. But this does not take place if we are just *along for the ride*.

These attitudes of waiting or searching for destiny are obviously not limited to relationships. For those who hold to the *on the hunt* model of destiny, life is continually lived in the future. They are never fully content with the present because their destiny lies somewhere just in front of them, and if they take their eyes off it for too long, they may miss out on what they believe God is trying to reveal to them. Before long, every present person, thing, and task loses real value and simply becomes a "northern star" that points toward the real goal. However, just as relationships are not meant to be rungs on a ladder that help us reach our destiny, neither is life meant to be lived fully for the future.

What about hope? Isn't this a living for the future? No! Though some have made it that. Many Christians have turned heaven into their destiny and, thus, their ultimate goal. They live in escape mode, just waiting for this hellish world to pass away so they can be in paradise. This *along for the ride* mind-set forgets about the present. It forgets about the hurting. It forgets about the responsibility laid upon us by Christ. It forgets to love along the way. In the already-not-yet kingdom inaugurated by Christ, the hope of God's future restoration has moved into the present. Christ has brought the future nearer than ever before.

It is this very hope of the certainty of what is to be that allows us to live out justice and love and peace in the present. We are not called to live *for* the future; we are called to live *in* the future by living the future out in our present. He has not called us to search out or wait for our destiny; rather, he has called us to embrace our calling and actively choose to love people in the present.

How, Then, Should We Pray?

In an interview with *Time* magazine, Rabbi Kushner referenced a study in which two groups of patients were in similar hospital settings. The only variable between the two groups was that one group was prayed for and the other was not. In the end, the study concluded that prayer seemed to have no influence on the recovery of the patients. Kushner went on to say, "God's job is not to make sick people healthy. That's the doctors' job. God's job is to make sick people brave."[8] He suggests that in Western society, we confuse God with Santa Claus. We believe that prayer means making a list of everything we want and trying to persuade God that we are entitled to it. According to Kushner, we have too often confused prayer with "bargaining with God."[9]

Is Kushner correct that most people see prayer as a way of bargaining with God to get what they want? Is this actually a bad thing? Scripture does call us to prayer (2 Chron. 7:14) and says God will give us whatever we ask if we believe (Matt. 21:22) and ask in his name (John 14:14; 1 John 5:14-15), right? Here is the problem with this line of thinking.

First, it pulls passages like these out of their contexts and ignores what they are really saying. Second, it does not actually take the time to consider the implications of this way of thinking. What does this say about this God? What does it say about Christianity and its purposes? Remember, we do not serve a manipulable God who can be controlled by saying the right words or doing the right things. When we reduce prayer to an exchange, we reduce God. Furthermore, when we reduce Christianity to an exchange, we get a worthless religion that models the consumerism of our society and does not actually help anyone.

It's starting to sound as if the stance against the manipulable God is contradictory to the stance *for* the God who can be wrestled with from chapter 3, but it isn't. The stories about Jacob, Moses, and Job are not about these guys manipulating God or getting their own way. These stories are about those who are so committed to the relationship that they are willing to stand toe to toe and cry out to this God; they are willing to doubt and lament and get angry, not because they want some consumerist exchange, but because they want God. They are ultimately acts of commitment and submission, not acts of control or manipulation.

Notice that in each of these three stories, God is moved to action, but he is moved by love, not manipulation. Furthermore, these movements are relational in purpose and action. God is moved to bless Jacob, but the blessing is not material; it is the blessing of helping Jacob embrace his true self and be transformed. Likewise, in Moses's situation, God is moved to relinquish his anger, which helps Moses know the heart of God and realize the depth of God's love for God's people. Finally, Job's wrestling prayers move God to reveal his true character, power, and presence to Job, which transform Job's outlook on his own situation.

Herein we see the primary purpose and power of prayer. God is too good and too loving just to give us what we want. Instead, God gives us what we need, and what we need is transformation. In their work on prayer, *Becoming the Answer to Our Prayers*, Shane Claiborne and Jonathan Wilson-Hartgrove, two urban activists in the new monastic movement, suggest that prayer is essential for the Christian, not only for the way it builds our relationship with God but also for the way it can move us to become the answers to our own prayers. In response to the common question voiced toward God, "Why don't you do something?" they suggest that God's response is, "I did do something. I made you."[10] Thus, they suggest, "Prayer is not so much about convincing God to do what we want God to do as it is about convincing ourselves to do what God wants us to do."[11]

As we said in our first book, *The Samaritan Project*, God's peace "transforms the way we pray, moving us away from asking God to change the world so that we get what we want to asking God to change us so that the world gets what it needs."[12] It is a dynamic synergism, whereby through prayer, God transforms us so we can transform the world. This does not remove God from the picture; God is the ultimate power behind our actions and will eventually transform everything. Yet God invites us to participate now. How awesome is that!

This brings us back to the prayer scriptures we cited above (2 Chron. 7:14; Matt. 21:22; John 14:14; 1 John 5:14-15). Each of these statements, in its context, speaks about God's transformation in us. They speak about God changing our attitudes to reflect his attitude. They speak of relationship, and they speak of action.

Trust in the LORD and do good;

dwell in the land and enjoy safe pasture.

Take delight in the LORD,

and he will give you the desires of your heart. (Ps. 37:3-4)

As we dwell in God and do good, God's desires become our desires. Therefore, what God gives us is God's very heart for others and the opportunities to choose God's ways in the present. This is why we must "pray without ceasing" (1 Thess. 5:17, KJV), because our transformation depends on our connection to God, and in many ways, so does the world's.

The Power of Choices

In his book *Chasing Daylight*, Erwin McManus makes a bold claim:

The most spiritual activity you will engage in today is making choices. All the other activities that we describe as spiritual—worship, prayer, meditation—are there to connect us to God and prepare us to live. While moments are the context within which we live, choices chart the course and determine the destination. . . .

. . . Our choices either move us toward God and all the pleasure that comes in Him or steer us away from Him to a life of shame and fear.[13]

Are our choices really the most spiritual activity in which we engage? Most of us probably do not view choices as spiritual acts, especially small choices. In fact, most of us hardly think about the small choices. We fall into daily routines, moving from point A to point B. After a while, even complex tasks can be performed on autopilot. However, we miss important opportunities when we cruise through life, and not just opportunities to stop and smell the roses. We are speaking of the kinds of opportunities to share the sacrificial love of God, to evidence God's abundant grace, and to reveal the already-not-yet kingdom to the world.

Jesus's Sermon on the Mount (Matt. 5–7) is a perfect example of the choices that lie before us, and the opportunity to bring those potential moments to life. However, much depends on the lens through which we read this powerful sermon. These are not mere words of exhortation. They are not simply ethical prose. They are an audible description of a new reality in which Christ's kingdom is being evidenced through the everyday choices of average individuals and groups as they live empowered by the Holy Spirit.

The Sermon on the Mount begins with the Beatitudes (5:3-10), a series of eight blessings that declare this new reality. The first and last ones—"Blessed are the poor in spirit" (v. 3) and "Blessed are those who are persecuted because of righteousness" (v. 10)—both conclude with these words: "for theirs is the kingdom of heaven." Yet this new kingdom reality, which is spoken of in the present tense, does not seem to have come to fruition. Why is this? Is Jesus wrong? Alternatively, does Matthew misquote Jesus and these statements are supposed to be in the future tense? No! Jesus was beginning to reveal the mystery of this new reality to the disciples and to the crowd, and in the same way, we, too, must catch a vision for this upside-down, countercultural kingdom, where the things we see every day are not as they seem; where the poor in spirit, as well as the materially poor (cf. Luke 6:20), along with those who are being persecuted, are considered blessed.

This does not mean they enjoy their current situations, nor does it mean we must seek out poverty or persecution. Rather, it means that those who have recognized Jesus as King and have entered the new kingdom reality are already part of the blessings of God. The hope of the future has been brought near and has given us a new perspective from which to view life in the present.

The other six Beatitudes (5:4-9) continue to explicate the alternativeness of the kingdom while simultaneously revealing the not-yet aspect. Each of these six blessings is followed by a future tense verb that shows that the fullness of the kingdom is yet to come. However, as the rest of the Sermon on the Mount makes clear, the kingdom continues to unfold and expand as God's people begin to embrace their new reality and, with it, their new identity. Kingdom people are being transformed into the image of their King.

However, this transformation is not so much about going to church every Sunday or reading our Bibles daily. It is not about saying prayers a certain way or singing the right songs. All these things can be important parts of worship if we allow them to shape us and focus us into the type of people who then go into our world and make choices that bring life and love rather than death and hatred. This is where McManus's words ring so true. The acts we traditionally attribute to being worship prepare us for the spiritual act of making choices!

Remember Jesus's parable concerning the sheep and the goats in Matthew 25:31-46? While it is a parable about the final judgment, it discloses important truths about the present. Listen to the opening words:

> Then the King will say to those on his right, "Come, you who are blessed by my Father; take your inheritance, the kingdom prepared for you since the creation of the world." (V. 34)

Notice that the reward is not the blessing. They are already considered blessed before they receive this reward. Instead, they are blessed because they are already part of the kingdom people and already serving the King by feeding the hungry, giving drink to the thirsty, taking in the stranger, clothing the naked, looking after the sick, and visiting the prisoner (vv. 35-39). They make choices to live out Christ's love in their world and, in so doing, love and worship God (cf. 22:37-39).

Returning to the Beatitudes, some questions begin to surface as this new kingdom reality is revealed to us. How are those who mourn comforted? How do the meek inherit the earth? How are those who hunger and thirst for righteousness filled, or the merciful shown mercy? How do the pure in heart see God, and who calls the peacemakers children of God? While the ultimate answer is that God does all these things at the consummation of the age, when Christ returns to make all things new, another answer begins to surface as we read this sermon. The people of the kingdom choose to do these things because it is part of who they are and who they are becoming.

We are the salt of the earth and the light of the world (5:13-16). We are those who embrace not the letter of the law but the love of the law (vv. 17-20). We seek not just to abolish murder but also to abolish hate (vv. 21-26), not just to do away with adultery but also to let go of lust (vv. 27-32). We live lives of integrity (vv. 33-37) and self-sacrifice (vv. 38-42). We love unconditionally, even our enemies, and in so doing, we are being made perfect, whole, and holy (vv. 43-48). We give without seeking reward (6:1-4), pray without seeking attention (vv. 5-15), and fast without seeking accolade (vv. 16-18). And because we serve only one master (vv. 19-24), and know this master to be the ultimate provider, we relinquish worry (vv. 25-34). Instead, our focus is on being transformed rather than on judging (7:1-6), on treating others as we want to be treated (vv. 7-12), and on walking the path of true life so our lives bear the fruit of genuine discipleship (vv. 13-23). We daily choose to build our present lives on the solid rock of Christ and his already-not-yet kingdom (vv. 24-27).

In other words, we are not searching out our destiny or waiting for our destiny to find us. Rather, we choose to live in a new reality in which desire, and not destiny, moves us. We desire to be like the King, and he transforms our worldly desires into kingdom desires!

Questions for Further Reflection or Small Group Discussion

1. When was the last time you heard the term *soul mates*? What was the setting?

2. Why do you think the idea of Mr. or Miss Right is so popular?

3. When was the last time you felt that something in your life could be described as inevitable?

4. React to the following quote from Rabbi Kushner: "God's job is not to make sick people healthy. That's the doctors' job. God's job is to make sick people brave."

5. What do you think about Claiborne and Wilson-Hartgrove's suggestion that prayer is about "convincing ourselves to do what God wants us to do"?

6. Do you agree with Erwin McManus that choices are our "most spiritual activity"?

7. Read the Beatitudes in Matthew 5:3-10. Which of these is easiest to embrace as a present reality in our world? Which is the hardest to embrace?

For Further Study

Beginner to Intermediate

Claiborne, Shane, and Jonathan Wilson-Hartgrove. *Becoming the Answer to Our Prayers: Prayers for Ordinary Radicals.* Downers Grove, IL: InterVarsity Press, 2008.

Fringer, Rob A., and Jeff K. Lane. *The Samaritan Project.* Kansas City: House Studio, 2012.

Greig, Pete. *God on Mute: Engaging the Silence of Unanswered Prayer.* Ventura, CA: Regal Books, 2007.

Lewis, C. S. *Letters to Malcolm: Chiefly on Prayer.* New York: Mariner Books, 2002.

More Advanced

Boyd, Gregory A. *God of the Possible: A Biblical Introduction to the Open View of God.* Grand Rapids: Baker, 2000.

Hauerwas, Stanley. *Matthew.* Brazos Theological Commentary on the Bible. Grand Rapids: Brazos Press, 2006.

McKnight, Scot. *Sermon on the Mount.* The Story of God Bible Commentary. Grand Rapids: Zondervan, 2013.

8

GOD TOLD ME TO

● ● ●

"God Told Me Too"

"Hey, Cora, I need to tell you something."

"Okay, what do you need to tell me, Gregg?"

"I was praying, and God told me to quit my job and start my own business. He told me to trust him and he would provide."

"That's interesting, Gregg, because God told me to—"

"He told you the same thing?!"

"No, you didn't let me finish my sentence. God didn't tell me *too*; God told me *to* . . . t-o . . . tell you that we have a mortgage and three kids to support and that you should listen to your wife. He said that when he wants you to do something, he will tell me too!"

This humorous fictional account is not difficult to imagine. In fact, a recent survey found that 38 percent of Americans have done something because they believed God told them to, with the largest percentage of these people (65 percent) claiming to be born-again Christians.[1] When was the last time you heard someone say God told him or her to do something? Were you skeptical? Did it involve you? When was the last time you said these words? What was the reaction?

"God told me to" has had a profound impact on the lives of many people throughout history, both positive and negative. Terrorists, presidents, sports stars, politicians, murderers, religious leaders, and many others have used these words as validation of divine authority for their actions. While we believe that God calls people to live a certain way in the world, we do not believe every action is part of God's desires. In a world where anyone can claim he or she is doing God's will, how do we decide what we are supposed to be doing? For those who believe God has called them to something, how can they judge whether their sense of divine revelation is in line with Scripture and with God's historic tendencies?

It has been our position that a theology of luck requires a newfound sense of responsibility and human participation in God and God's mission in the world. If this is true, then we must all discover God's calling, not just for the church, but we ought to make sure each of us is being responsible with all that God desires for us.

Our Primary Calling

The concept of *calling* is found throughout Scripture, usually in reference to God calling someone to a specific task or mission. So, for instance, God calls Abram to leave his family and security and move to an unknown place. He calls Moses to return to Egypt and liberate the Israelites. He calls David to unite and build a kingdom and Jeremiah to speak challenging words in the midst of exile. Likewise, Jesus calls the disciples to follow him and then, later, to carry out his mission; and he calls the apostle Paul to be his missionary to the Gentiles.

In all these callings, we see God at work, wooing and persuading people toward specific actions. Yet it is often difficult to compare ourselves to biblical characters and their situations. Does God still call us to specific things today? Moreover, does God clearly make it known? Will we all get our own personal burning bush or Damascus road experience?

Though God still does reveal himself in dynamic ways, we often forget that we now live in the age of the Holy Spirit, which means God usually speaks to us internally, through the Spirit, rather than externally, through some spectacular phenomenon. In addition, God has given believers gifts of the Spirit. These various gifts are not given so we can elevate ourselves or fulfill our own dreams and desires. Instead, they are to be used for the "common good" (1 Cor. 12:7) and for uniting and building up the body in love (Eph. 4:12-16). God has also made us each unique and given us certain abilities, talents, and passions. These, too, are to be used for the common good and for building up the body. It is not as if spiritual gifts are for the church and the other things for our own personal gain. All of who we are is supposed to be a divine expression of God's magnificence and love to our world.

This is clearly seen in Genesis 1:26-28, which speaks of humanity's creation.

Then God said, "Let us make mankind in our image, in our likeness, so that they may rule over the fish in the sea and the birds in the sky, over the livestock and all the wild animals, and over all the creatures that move along the ground."

So God created mankind in his own image,

in the image of God he created them;

male and female he created them.

God blessed them and said to them, "Be fruitful and increase in number; fill the earth and subdue it. Rule over the fish in the sea and the birds in the sky and over every living creature that moves on the ground."

We were created in the image and likeness of God, and our first calling is to reflect God. Likewise, we are called to fill, subdue, and rule over God's creation. These three verbs (and especially the last two) are often mishandled because they are taken out of their narrative context and used to promote ungodly acts of human subjugation. However, this is not what the narrative intends; it is not a divine mandate to control or manipulate others. Instead, within the context, we see that God invites us to reflect God's image and actions. Just as God created the world, God calls us to be part of the creation process through populating the earth.

This intent and call are made clear in Genesis 5:1-3, where Adam's genealogy begins with a recounting of Genesis 1:27, followed by the report that Adam "had a son in his own likeness, in his own image" (5:3). Likewise, just as God subdued the chaos (as we discussed in chap. 3), God calls us to subdue the earth; God calls us to keep the chaos at bay through our filling of the earth and, moreover, through our proper ruling over creation. Therefore, *ruling*, properly understood, speaks of stewardship and partnership. God calls us together to participate in ruling over his creation, but since it still belongs to God, we are merely stewards of it.

We are called to steward in a way that reflects the very heart and character of God, which means the picture of God to which one subscribes has a profound impact on how one stewards. We probably do not need to search very hard for examples of Christians ruling through either ignoring or controlling. The former are indifferent and abdicate all responsibility; the latter wield power over people, forcing them into submission, often through shame and guilt.

However, what would our stewarding look like if we were to embrace the loving God who creates humanity for relationship and, thus, with free will/free grace? What if we were to emulate the kind of Father who yields power to creation through the giving of the Holy Spirit and who actively participates in creation through the incarnation of the Son? We cannot tell you exactly what it would look like, since it would look different for each person and each situation. Yet we can tell you, in general terms, that it would be an engaging and relational type of stewarding that took all of creation into consideration. It would involve freeing people to be themselves while walking alongside them through good and bad. It would be governed by genuine love and motivated by the hope of transformation. Oh yes, and it would be the kind of stewardship that often requires personal sacrifice and often encounters personal suffering.

We can now see that these two callings of reflecting the image of God and stewarding God's creation are actually one and the same, and we refer to it as our *primary calling*. It is an invitation to share in the very nature and mission of God in the world. Every Christian's call (and, ideally, every human's call) is not a self-seeking call but a self-surrendering call to love our world and the people in it the same way God loves creation, and in this way we are also loving God (cf. Matt. 25:31-45).

The Great Commandment of Matthew 22:37-39 is in fact a summation of our primary calling. Likewise, since God's mission is to transform all humanity through God's love, and since discipleship is part of the transformation process, the Great Commission of Matthew 28:19-20 can also be viewed as a summation of this primary calling.

This is not just a call for pastors and priests, nor is it just for the really spiritual believers. It is a call for all Christians, both as a collective and as individuals. Though it may sound general, it is also very specific. Each of us must ask whether we as individuals and we as communities of Christ followers reflect the image of God in everything we do, say, and think. We must question whether our stewarding mirrors God's loving heart. Furthermore, we must begin to recognize that every other calling we have in life is, first and foremost, governed by this primary calling.

Occupational Calling

Whenever someone strikes up a conversation with a stranger, it is not long before the "What do you do?" question surfaces. This question exemplifies the modern tendency to equate *calling* with one's *occupation*. While these two ideas are not synonymous, they are interconnected, and the former governs the latter. In a very real way, our occupation should be an important part of our calling. Think about it: In the course of an average person's life, conservatively speaking, he or she will spend 8 hours a day, 5 days a week, 48 weeks a year (assuming 4 weeks off for public holidays and vacation), for a minimum of 47 years (assuming he or she works full-time from the ages of 18 to 65) at work. That equates to 90,240 hours, or 10.3 years! This makes the question of what God wants me to do for a career that much more important. We do not think God created work because God was looking for something to fill the time or to distract us. Instead, work becomes another place for us to live out our primary calling.

As you might already have guessed, we do not believe there is one specific career path for which we are destined. In a theology of luck, God's vision for our lives is less a journey of inevitability and more a journey of discovery and response. However, this journey must be a conscious choice that aligns with our primary calling. Frederick Buechner, in his book *Wishful Thinking*, offers a possible antidote for the confusing process of discovering God's desires for our lives:

> There are all different kinds of voices calling you to all different kinds of work, and the problem is to find out which is the voice of God rather than of Society, say, or the Superego, or Self-Interest.
>
> . . . The kind of work God usually calls you to is the kind of work *(a)* that you need most to do and *(b)* that the world most needs to have done. If you [find your work rewarding], you've presumably met requirement *(a)*, but if your work [does not benefit others], the chances are you've missed requirement *(b)*. On the other hand, if your work [does benefit others], you have probably met requirement

(b), but if most of the time you're [unhappy with] it, the chances are you have not only bypassed *(a)* but probably aren't helping your [customers] much either.

. . . The place God calls you to is the place where your deep gladness and the world's deep hunger meet.[2]

These two criteria for discovering our occupational calling are profound and highlight the reality that God's love is both universal and particular. Each of us has specific talents and passions, which God wants us to live into because this is how God created us. God is not a sadistic God who creates us one way and then does not allow us to act in this way. Rather, God is a loving God who finds joy in our joy but who also knows us so intimately that God knows the only thing that will bring us real joy is being transformed into God's image through the living out of our primary calling.

This is where the second aspect comes. God has called us to participate in God's mission, which means finding ways to serve and love others in everything we do, absolutely including our occupation. We must not approach the choice of occupation lightly. We live in a world that values occupation and takes it seriously. We must, too, but not for the same reasons. It is not about power, prestige, or money. It is not about self-gain or even familial gain. As Christians, our occupations are extensions of our primary calling. They are an opportunity for us to evidence our God-given passions, talents, and gifts as well as ways to reveal God's love, mercy, grace, and justice to our world. God has freed us to choose, but this choice cannot be made arbitrarily. Our freedom to choose our occupation cannot be seen as the power to live selfishly but, rather, as the freedom to learn God's dreams for the world and find a way to embody them through all we do.

Learning God's dream for the world requires that we take two things seriously when making the decision. First, we must take ourselves seriously. We must spend time discovering who we truly are, who God has made us to be. What are our talents? What gifts has God given us? What are we passionate about? We cannot allow the world to define these things. The world did not create our "inmost being" or "knit [us] together in [our] mother's womb" (Ps. 139:13). God did this, and it is only through spending time with God that we can discover who we truly are *in* God. As we said in the last chapter, this is an important aspect of prayer. As we grow in relationship with God, we not only understand God better but also understand ourselves better. This may or may not change our passions, but one thing it will surely do is focus our passions so they can be used for God's glory.

The second thing we must take seriously is our world. We will not know the "world's deep hunger" if we do not spend time living in and viewing our world. This means we cannot have an escapist mind-set. Nor can we view the world from our own limited perspective or from the world's perspective. Instead, we must view the world from God's perspective, from the perspective of the kingdom. It is only here that we will be able to move past our prejudices, presuppositions, and judgments to see the places of deep pain and need as well as the places of true beauty. It is here that we will find the intersection of our passion and the world's need. It is here that we will catch the glorious vision of our occupational calling.

While we have painted a rather picturesque scene whereby each of us consciously works with God to discover our occupational callings, we know that not everyone is fully given this choice. Based on the places and situations in which we were born, how we were raised, and our current environments, we may have little choice about what we do. Some people are forced, by others or their situations, to work jobs that bring them little joy, for which they have little passion and for which they may or may not have talents and gifts. Furthermore, we recognize that some may find themselves in jobs that, at first glance, do not appear to meet the second criterion, while still being much-needed jobs. Does this mean they are unable to fully live out the lives God desires for them?

We must emphatically say no! This would be not only a sad situation for them but also a sad commentary on the God who created them. Remember, calling and occupation are not synonyms. Those who find themselves choiceless in their occupations are still called by God to live out their primary callings. Additionally, the attitude in which they approach their jobs, the way they carry out their jobs, and the way they interact with others at their jobs are all choices they *do* have, and choices that can benefit the worlds around them. They may need to seek out other ways to live out their passions, but that doesn't mean they can't also come to find some gladness and sense of calling in their occupations. In the words of the apostle Paul, "Whatever you do, whether in word or deed, do it all in the name of the Lord Jesus, giving thanks to God the Father through him" (Col. 3:17).

This also means that while we may have the choice to do nothing with our lives, as Christians this is actually not an option. We are not speaking about those who are unable to work due to their physical or mental states, or due to certain, unavoidable circumstances. We are simply stating that those who are able to work must do so. The definition of *work* here is not one so narrow to exclude volunteer roles or other nonpaying positions. The definition of *work* is very broad indeed. Not to use the gifts God has given us is a waste of those gifts, talents, and passions, speaks volumes about our faith (see 2 Thess. 3:6-15), and, sadly, also reflects negatively on our God. Cornelius Plantinga, in his book *Not the Way It's Supposed to Be*, offers us this sober warning:

> Making a career of Nothing—wandering through malls, killing time, making small talk, watching television programs until we know their characters better than our own children—robs the community of our gifts and energies and shapes life into a yawn at the God and savior of the world. The person who will not bestir herself, the person who hands himself over to Nothing, in effect says to God: you have made nothing of interest and redeemed no one of consequence, including me.[3]

Let us conclude this section with a few more points about occupational calling that we were not able to explore here:

1. Some occupations will never meet the second criterion and, as such, should not be occupations in which Christians partake (e.g., professions that are illegal or seek to purposely manipulate or cheat people).

2. Even when a person finds an occupation that meets both criteria, this does not guarantee smooth sailing or mean there will not be struggles and sacrifices along the way.

3. In our occupations, we must stay connected to God, relying on God's strength to maintain a Christlike attitude and the motivation of love. Although we may move through many different careers, our primary calling remains the same.

4. There may be times when we are presented with two equally good job choices that meet both criteria. In such cases, it is doubtful whether God really cares which one we choose as long as we represent God well in the one we do choose.

5. Our choice of occupational fields or of particular jobs should rarely be made alone. Since we work for the good of the body, we should allow others in the community of faith to help guide us in our decision making.

6. If you want to see some examples of occupational calling that take Buechner's two criteria seriously, check out Scott Harrison, CEO and founder of Charity: Water;[4] Greg Haugen, CEO and founder of International Justice Mission;[5] and Jessica Jackley, cofounder of Kiva.[6]

Discerning Together

The idea that partnership with God is simultaneously partnership with the body of Christ has huge implications in all areas of our lives, including the *God told me to* moments. The Bible teaches us that discernment is most often a community affair. Even some of the strongest figures seek guidance from others when it comes to big decisions. For instance, Moses receives guidance from his father-in-law, Jethro, shortly after coming out of Egypt, and the issue is actually about choosing capable leaders to help handle disputes and make judgments for the people who are seeking God's will (Exod. 18). Likewise, Paul and Barnabas seek the assurance of the leaders in Jerusalem concerning their mission to the Gentiles (Gal. 2:1-10; cf. Acts 15:1-21).

Perhaps the best example is the often quoted and misrepresented words of Paul in Romans 12:1-2.

Therefore, I exhort you all, brothers and sisters, through the mercies of God to present all your bodies as a (united) living sacrifice, as holy and pleasing to God, as your reasonable act of service; and all of you are not to be conformed to this age, but rather you all are to be transformed (together), having a (united) renewed mind, so that together you all discern the will of God—the good and the pleasing and the perfect.[7]

This translation allows us to see that Paul instructs the community as a whole, not just individuals. As the body of Christ, we are called to come together and present ourselves to God as a single, united, living sacrifice. This means that while we each have a responsibility to take part in the offering, we form one beautiful and acceptable sacrifice to God. Worship unites us as nothing else can. In our own strength and as individuals, it is impossible to be holy and pleasing to God, and yet, through the mercies of God, together we are holy and pleasing to God just as we are being made holy and pleasing to God.

Some translations read, "This is your spiritual act of worship" (e.g., NIV). The word *spiritual* is more accurately translated "reasonable" or "rational." We tend to overspiritualize things to the point that they become purely religious rituals or emotionally led actions. There is a place for these things, but here, Paul is speaking about consciously thinking through an act before it is performed. It is not about moving through the motions or waiting until we feel a certain way before we act. Rather, we are called to come together as believers and process together what our offerings to God are going to be.

It becomes a "reasonable act of worship" because it is not made by one individual acting on his or her own authority; rather, it is made by a group of believers working together to offer an acceptable sacrifice that not only glorifies their God but that also fits their context. It is reasonable, meaning that it is not unbearable or unmanageable because we bear the responsibility and the burden together. Moreover, because it is reasonable, we are called together to perform this act of service regularly. This is why we are "living" rather than "dead." Our sacrifice is not a onetime offering of ourselves but a daily act of commitment and community.

The passage goes on to say that just as we come together to become a united, living sacrifice, we are also called to be transformed together into a single and united, renewed mind. Does that mean we cease to think for ourselves and are morphed into some giant brain that makes all the decisions for us? Well, not exactly. The renewed mind Paul speaks of is an invitation to share in the same attitudes and actions of Christ (see Phil. 2:5). It is a reminder that as those who are in Christ and who are filled with the Holy Spirit, "we have the mind of Christ" (1 Cor. 2:16). Christ is our head (Col. 1:18), and we are his body. The two go hand in hand. Just as we cannot be the body by ourselves, we cannot have the mind of Christ as individuals. These realities do not belong to any one person but are limited to the community as a whole, "so that together you all discern the will of God." We do not have to wander aimlessly, searching for the will of God. Scripture tells us that as we are united, we are able to discern God's will together and it will be good, pleasing, and perfect. This speaks volumes of the confidence God has in God's church and the authority God gives us. This interpretation of Romans 12:1-2 is validated in the words of Jesus in Matthew 18:19-20:

> Again, truly I tell you that if two of you on earth agree about anything they ask for, it will be done for them by my Father in heaven. For where two or three gather in my name, there am I with them.

These are not words about prayer; they are words about the authority God has granted God's church. When we come together and agree, God is in our midst, giving us wisdom and helping us to reveal God's kingdom discernment here on earth. However, such power is only possible when we as individuals and as the church model the same kind of power as Christ, the same type of ruling, the same type of love! It is not that we stop thinking for ourselves; it is that we stop thinking only *about* ourselves. It is not that we become mindless; it is that we mind the other. This community perspective, which is actually a kingdom perspective, allows us to see a much larger picture of what is going on. We are not limited by the blind spots that our circumstances so often create. Nor are we led astray by our selfishness, selfishness that is not often evident to us.

Rather, we are able to see much more clearly everything that is going on. We are able to openly ask questions and have questions asked of us. We are able to bring our fears and doubts to the table and have valid ones confirmed and wrong ones gently dismissed. Moreover, we are able to move more confidently forward, knowing that others have made the decisions with us and walk beside us through them and through their consequences. We know this picture is overly optimistic and idealistic, but so is the kingdom; and this kingdom beckons us to shine like stars so that all may see God's glory.

We hope you are beginning to see that a theology of luck says it is our responsibility and calling to act a certain way in the world, to invest our lives in one another, and to live out our primary calling in everything we are and do. God has not abandoned us to destiny but has invited us to partner together with God and God's mission in this world. To be obedient to God requires embracing God's desires and learning to make them our own. Next time we sense God calling us in a certain direction, we should check this against our primary calling and bring it before other believers for discernment.

Be assured, we do not walk this journey alone. We do not have to carry all the burdens. We do not have to be the savior of the world. Instead, we walk together and reflect the Savior *to* our world. This is God's will!

Questions for Further Reflection
or Small Group Discussion

1. When was the last time you heard someone say that God told him or her to do something?
2. Have you ever told someone that God called you to do something? What was the reaction you received?
3. What is your favorite story of God calling someone to a certain action in the Bible?
4. Do you have an event that you see as your own personal burning bush?
5. What do you think it means to be made in the image of God?
6. How did you choose the career you now have? Do you believe God guided you to your current occupation?
7. React to this quote: "To be obedient to God requires embracing God's desires and learning to make them our own."

For Further Study

Beginner to Intermediate

Bonhoeffer, Dietrich. *Life Together*. Translated by John W. Doberstein. New York: HarperCollins, 1954.

Buechner, Frederick. *Wishful Thinking: A Seeker's ABC*. San Francisco: HarperCollins, 1993.

Witherington, Ben, III. *Work: A Kingdom Perspective on Labor*. Grand Rapids: Eerdmans, 2011.

More Advanced

Banks, Robert. *Paul's Idea of Community*. Rev. ed. Peabody, MA: Hendrickson Publishing, 1994.

Brower, Kent. *Living As God's Holy People: Holiness and Community in Paul.* Milton Keynes, UK: Paternoster, 2010.

Flemming, Dean. *Recovering the Full Mission of God: A Biblical Perspective on Being, Doing and Telling.* Downers Grove, IL: InterVarsity Press, 2013.

9

GOD'S DREAM AND OUR PURPOSE

● ● ●

God's Desire

In the 2003 movie *Bruce Almighty*,[1] we meet Bruce, a small-time reporter who has temporarily been given God's power. At first, he is delighted by this newfound ability, but then he realizes it also comes with the responsibility of answering everyone's prayers. His elation quickly disperses as he becomes completely overwhelmed by the billions of unrelenting prayers. To stop the noise, Bruce decides to simply give people what they want, thinking this will make them happy. However, as you can imagine, such a solution causes even more problems. Bruce sees firsthand the chaos and dystopia that is created when everyone gets what he or she desires.

Unable to make things right, Bruce seeks out the real God, played by Morgan Freeman, for advice. The character of God—

who, either ironically or fittingly, is dressed as a janitor—invites Bruce to join him in some janitorial service and share some perspective. After they have cleaned a large area, God says, "No matter how filthy something gets, you can always clean it right up."

Bruce admits, "There were so many. I just gave them all what they want."

God responds, "Yeah. But since when does anyone have a clue about what they want?"[2]

Then Bruce receives the following pep talk:

Parting your soup is not a miracle, Bruce. It's a magic trick. A single mom who's working two jobs and still finds time to take her kid to soccer practice, that's a miracle. A teenager who says "no" to drugs and "yes" to an education, that's a miracle. People want me to do everything for them, but what they don't realize is, they have the power. You want to see a miracle, son? Be the miracle.[3]

Morgan Freeman's character reveals a profound confidence in his creation. In this make-believe world, human beings have been empowered to do more than they realize they can do. While there is the awareness that most people do not actually know what they want, there is also the revelation that when they, like the single mom or the courageous teenager, do find something of purpose and meaning, they are empowered to carry out these everyday miracles and that this is actually part of God's desire for them.

Is this idea really make-believe? We don't think so. God has empowered creation, through the Holy Spirit, to carry out these everyday miracles. It is God's desire for humanity to participate in the process, and from start to finish, Scripture reveals this reality. Revelation 21:1-5 gives us a glorious vision of the fulfillment of God's restoration and re-creation project and the continuation of the grand narrative.

Then I saw "a new heaven and a new earth," for the first heaven and the first earth had passed away, and there was no longer any sea. I saw the Holy City, the new Jerusalem, coming down out of heaven from God, prepared as a bride beautifully dressed for her husband. And I heard a loud voice from the throne saying, "Look! God's dwelling place is now among the people, and he will dwell with them. They will be his people, and God himself will be with them and be their God. 'He will wipe every tear from their eyes. There will be no more death' or mourning or crying or pain, for the old order of things has passed away."

He who was seated on the throne said, "I am making everything new!"

We read these words and are immediately transported back to the garden of Eden. We are reminded of God's original intent for humanity to walk with God in intimate relationship. It is a picture of perfection, where the wrongs of sin are righted and the rights of love are no longer wronged. Where the chaos has been completely ordered, never to return. Where, rather than humanity going to heaven to be with God, God comes down from heaven to dwell forever with God's creation. Where the old order of things has passed away and, with them, death, mourning, crying, pain, injustice, shame, hate, lust, gossip, and all other things that are void of love.

The Revelation passage ends with the King proclaiming: "I am making everything new!" While much of the passage speaks about the future, this last line is written in the present tense. God is *currently* making everything new. However, we must not have too narrow a view of the present. These words were written nearly two thousand years ago to encourage Christians who faced persecution and who desperately needed to hear those words. That is to say, God has been carrying out God's restoration plan for some time now.

Can you see it? Most people do not. We read our history books and see war, famine, hate, and death. We look at the news today and see these same things. It does not appear that time is moving toward some final paradise but, rather, that time keeps repeating itself and, if anything, is moving toward some catastrophic destruction. We begin to assume, like historic Israel concerning the first coming, that all these things will take place at the second coming. All we can do at this point is trust and wait.

However, this is not the picture Scripture paints, nor is it the picture we have been painting. Rather, we learn repeatedly that God is already at work in the present bringing about God's kingdom. It's not being drawn out because God needs more time. This interim period represents God's grace and love; it is a time for people to discover the depths of God's love (2 Pet. 3:8-9).

It is also a time for God's people to participate in God's mission. God could have accomplished re-creation through any means, but God chose to use us. Therefore, it seems God's desire is not just restoration but also to see God's people being part of the restoration process. *We* are God's desire, and God's dream is our full participation. God's love for us is so great that God desires for us to freely choose to be transformed into God's image so we can be part of the transformation process of others and of our world. God is making everything new *through* us!

Freedom and Response

What is our responsibility with the freedom we have been given? What are the limitations of our freedom? Moreover, what *is* freedom? These are all important questions we must answer if we are to live out God's desire in the world. Dietrich Bonhoeffer gives profound insight into the phenomenon of freedom.

> Freedom is not a quality which can be revealed—it is not a possession, a presence, an object, nor is it a form for existence—but a relationship and nothing else. In truth, freedom is a relationship between two persons. Being free means "being free for the other," because the other has bound me to him. Only in relationship with the other am I free.[4]

For most, this radical definition sounds like the opposite of freedom. How can we be free if we are bound to the other? Furthermore, how is freedom not something we possess? This second question actually helps answer the first question. Freedom is not owned by any one person but, rather, is integrally tied to love and, thus, to God. True freedom is something in which humanity has been invited to participate. It is part of the grace of God. Yet, like love, freedom requires relationship.

Love requires at least two people. We cannot love by ourselves, and self-love conceived apart from the love of others is really just insecurity (this does not negate a proper valuing of oneself based on God's standards). As we have said multiple times, love is expansive and thus requires one to move outside oneself to embrace the other. In the same way, freedom is expansive, both requiring and considering other people. True freedom creates freedom for others, and any so-called freedom that takes another's freedom away is false.

An idealized concept of freedom pervades our world with the myth of autonomous liberty. However, if we spend any amount of time actually thinking about this, we will quickly recognize the impossibility of such a naïve notion. We can all recognize the interconnectedness between humans as well as the interconnectedness between humans and the rest of creation. As illustrated in chapter 2, the choices we make have consequences for others, just as the choices they make have consequences for us. Likewise, whether you believe in global warming, we all recognize that human choices have negatively and positively affected the rest of creation, both organic and inorganic. Therefore, freedom must mean more than just individual rights. From a kingdom perspective, freedom is not rights but responsibility. The irony of Christian freedom is that as we unite with Christ and his body, we actually freely surrender our freedom to the lordship of Christ.

One of Paul's favorite self-identifiers is "slave" (e.g., Rom. 1:1; Gal. 1:10; Titus 1:1). This is, understandably, not a term we like to use in our world; too much evil has been perpetrated under this label. Yet the Greek word *doulos* can also be translated "servant," a word that might help us better understand freedom as well as love. If you remember, Philippians 2:7 speaks of Christ taking the form of a servant (or slave) and of emptying himself. In other words, Christ uses his freedom for the sake of others. This is the ultimate picture of love, which reveals the true nature and character of God. Offering ourselves as servants of Christ is, therefore, not an act of bondage, but an act of freedom and love. The same is true when we empty ourselves of selfishness and allow God's Spirit to flow through us and enable us to love our world in concrete and tangible ways.

God does not force us to become his servants or to serve our world, but God does offer us this responsibility. Our response should be an act of freedom that is motivated by love. If we serve out of guilt or shame or obligation, it is not love. However, if we allow God's love to transform us from the inside out, then this ever-expansive love will naturally and freely flow out of us to our world. In the words of Paul, in 2 Corinthians 5:14-15:

> For Christ's love compels us, because we are convinced that one died for all, and therefore all died. And he died for all, that those who live should no longer live for themselves but for him who died for them and was raised again.

A perfect example of Christian freedom is seen in 1 Corinthians 8. The relatively young Corinthian church is divided over several issues, and here Paul deals with the problem of whether Christians can eat food that has been sacrificed to idols. Corinth has many pagan temples dedicated to various gods, and most of these temples practice some form of animal sacrifice or offering as part of the people's worship. With so many people and so many temples, even after some of the sacrifice is burnt up and the priests receive their portion, there is still an abundance of leftovers, among which can be found perfectly good meats, grains, and spices. These leftovers are often sold in the marketplace at a significantly lower price, a practice that provides a way for those of lower economic standing to afford these commodities.

The church in Corinth, which consists of people of varying economic status, is at odds over this issue. Some believe that "there is no God but one" (v. 4) and that, therefore, believers can consume such food with clear consciences. Others believe that since it has been offered to pagan gods, the food is defiled and should be avoided by believers.

Paul's opinion on the matter is mixed; he is able to see both viewpoints. Yet his exhortation to the community, in verses 9-13, is very clear:

Be careful, however, that the exercise of your rights does not become a stumbling block to the weak. For if someone with a weak conscience sees you, with all your knowledge, eating in an idol's temple, won't that person be emboldened to eat what is sacrificed to idols? So this weak brother or sister, for whom Christ died, is destroyed by your knowledge. When you sin against them in this way and wound their weak conscience, you sin against Christ. Therefore, if what I eat causes my brother or sister to fall into sin, I will never eat meat again, so that I will not cause them to fall.

From Paul's perspective, the issue is not food sacrificed to idols, or whether a person has the freedom to partake of such food. Rather, the issue is relational. If someone's free choice causes another person to stumble or fall away from Christ, then that choice is sin, not only against that person but also against Christ. For the Christian, freedom must be responsive *and* responsible. In Christ, we are freer than we have ever been (cf. Rom. 6), yet we also have more responsibility than ever before. We no longer make myopic choices but must take the consequences of our choices more seriously.

How will this choice affect those around me? How will this decision reflect on the church and on Christ? Will this choice release love into the world? Will this choice bring justice? It requires not only self-awareness but also others-awareness. This is the kind of freedom to which we have been called, and this is the kind of love that is at work in us through the Holy Spirit. God has made us free for the other!

Purpose and Fulfillment

Throughout the book, we have made many claims related to our purpose and our responsibility. We have said we were created to be in relationship with Christ and created to love others. We have talked about God's desire for us to participate in God's mission to the world and about our primary calling of imitating God through our stewardship. Finally, we have spoken about the responsibility of freedom and choice. Together this sounds like an impossible task for anyone, and it is. This is because it is not a task for any *one* but a task for *everyone*. These things are God's desire for the world, and we, as the church, should already be evidencing them to our world. These things should not be viewed as commands. They are not a list of requirements that enable us to receive God's grace or make us worthy of God's love. Rather, we should think of them as divine invitations to live out our purpose.

There is a variety of interrelated biblical concepts used to speak about our purpose, but perhaps the most fitting is the often misunderstood word *perfection*. Contrary to popular belief, the biblical concept of perfection does not mean "without fault." Absolute perfection is attributed to God alone (Deut. 32:4). In the Old Testament, the most common Hebrew word for *perfect* is *tamim*, which speaks of "wholeness" or "soundness." Likewise, in the New Testament, the Greek word *teleios* carries the meaning of "mature" or "complete." The idea of wholeness and completeness relative to humanity speaks to our purpose. We are whole when we are living in relationship with our Creator. We are complete when we are living the way we were created to live.

The story of the rich young ruler in Matthew 19:16-22 gives us insight into this concept. The young man comes to Jesus, asking, "Teacher, what good thing must I do to get eternal life?" (v. 16).

To which Jesus responds, "If you want to enter life, keep the commandments" (v. 17). Then Jesus adds, "If you want to be perfect [*teleios*], go, sell your possessions and give to the poor, and you will have treasure in heaven. Then come, follow me" (v. 21).

The difference between eternal life and perfection is the difference between salvation and purpose. Both are good, yet many settle for the first without realizing God offers the second. The second speaks to wholeness and completeness in the present. Jesus invites this young man to embrace more than just a list of dos and don'ts and to expect more than just a future salvation. He invites the man to a dynamic relationship in which he can live out his created purpose and find joy and fulfillment in the present while revealing the kingdom to others.

Biblical perfection should therefore be understood as relational. It reflects the transformation process that God desires to bring about in each of us as we freely surrender ourselves to God's love. First John 4:12 actually tells us that God wants to perfect his love in us. We have the freedom to make this decision. Perfection is not forced upon us. Rather, it is an important and intimate part of the relationship to which God invites us.

However, we must choose not only to enter this relationship but also to embrace the transformation that this relationship will inevitably create. The reality is, wherever God is allowed, transformation takes place. This is why God keeps showing up. This is why God is so persistent in his pursuit of us. God knows the power of his presence to transform, and he continually offers this presence to us in the hope that we will embrace it and remain in it long enough to begin reflecting God's perfection (Matt. 5:48). In the words of William Greathouse, "Perfection is a life of dedication and constancy in fellowship with the Almighty."[5]

Yet this decision does not come without cost; living out our purpose will be difficult and painful, and like the rich young ruler, many will walk away. Transformation is the process of shedding the consequences of our sinful choices and the consequences of others' sins, both of which have formed us into the kind of people we are today—those who are trapped by their own limited worldview and their own selfish desires; those molded by guilt and shame; those imprisoned by insecurity and therefore unable to imagine a God as loving as the one Scripture reveals; those so consumed by anger and hate that they hurt themselves and others; those broken by disappointment but lashing out at the hands who seek to help. Just as it took years to make us into these people, it takes years to transform us into people who reflect God's image.

Why go through this process if it will be so difficult and painful? Why take on these responsibilities? It comes down to our understanding of purpose. Purpose equals fulfillment. It is only as we live out our purpose that we will find deep joy. It is only as we embrace the process of being made perfect that we will begin to better understand God, our world, and ourselves. It is only through transformation that we will begin living out God's desire and dream and that we will be beneficial to this world.

What Now?

This book has been an attempt to deconstruct inconsistent and unhealthy pictures of God that have led to inconsistent and unhealthy followers of God. It is our hope that the God of relationship we have revealed is more consistent and provides a foundation for Christians to better understand their purpose and better love their world. A system that is fully controlled does not allow for choice, luck, or responsibility; whereas, a system that allows for luck also allows for genuine love, free response, and actual responsibility. In essence, we cannot have one without the other. We may be more comfortable believing that God controls every minute detail and that nothing is left to chance. Yet many have sought to follow this kind of God while insisting they have free will and are thus responsible for their actions. Only a relational God creates out of love and *for* love and, thus, creates humanity with the ability to choose.

This type of creation inevitably brings the possibility of luck, both good and bad.

We have come to see and believe that a theology of luck allows us the freedom to move beyond a world that is fully ordained and manipulated. A theology of luck also allows for love and reveals a vision for our world; a vision created and empowered by God, in which we have the privilege and the responsibility to participate.

We know we have only touched the surface of these important issues, and it is our hope that it will begin conversations across the church. The end goal is a people who reflect the very nature and character of God in our world, but that must begin with a proper picture of God. For this reason, we want to end this book with one very practical step that will move us further on the journey toward discovering the nature of God and our calling. It will then move us into our world in tangible ways to live out our purpose and therein find joy and fulfillment and bring these same things to our world.

A Hermeneutic of Love

One of the most important elements in moving forward on the Christian journey is the disciplined and intentional reading of Scripture, both individually and as a community. Since our vision of God often determines how we live and act in this world, the disciplined and intentional reading of Scripture is especially important because it ultimately determines the way we view God. We want to suggest a particular method for reading the Bible that will help guide us toward a healthy and consistent end.

The word *hermeneutics* is derived from a Greek word meaning "translate" or "interpret." It is used by biblical scholars to speak about the science or art of biblical interpretation. It takes into account the three worlds of the Bible: (1) the world behind the text, which is focused on the authors and their historic settings; (2) the world in the text, which is focused on the literary text itself; and (3) the world in front of the text, which is focused on the reader.

This third world has only recently received the attention it deserves. While it is vital that we take all three worlds seriously in our attempts to understand, interpret, and apply Scripture, it is important to recognize that when we come to read and interpret Scripture, we come with particular assumptions, biases, beliefs, and backgrounds of our own. We read Scripture through a variety of lenses, whether knowingly or unknowingly, and these lenses ultimately guide our interpretation.

For instance, if a person has grown up with the teaching that the Bible says women are inferior to men, or women should not be in places of leadership in the church, that view will guide the way the person reads the rest of Scripture, and not just the few particular passages that deal with this issue. Unless the person is aware of this lens, it becomes difficult to give the issue a fair reading.

Generally, when encountering difficult passages, we should use the whole of Scripture as a control against creating inconsistencies. So if something is encountered on the surface of a scriptural passage that doesn't fall in line with the view of God that the rest of Scripture as a whole has established, it might be worth considering that the passage in question has more layers than the ones we see on the surface.

Similarly, if a person believes that the creation story in Genesis is a historical and scientific account rather than a faith assertion about this particular God, then the person will most likely interpret Genesis as well as the rest of Scripture in a particular way. Furthermore, this lens will also affect the person's understanding of the surrounding world and the "truth" that this world puts forth.

Here we can recognize the profound impact our biases can have not only on how we read the Bible but also on how we view and interpret our world. For this reason, it becomes imperative that each of us seeks to recognize and understand the various presuppositions we bring to Scripture. We are not saying these will all be negative. In fact, some are very positive if we remain aware of them.

In this book, we have described three different views of God, each leading to a specific theological understanding and a unique gospel perspective. Each of these three pictures of God also leads to a different hermeneutic lens through which it reads Scripture and understands the world.

The God of control, who manipulates every event in history, naturally leads to a theology of certainty. Furthermore, since we have no other option but to come along for the ride, we understand this God to offer a gospel of acquiescence. Finally, the God of control also moves us to take on a *hermeneutic of authority*.

The hermeneutic of authority views Scripture through the lens of power. As such, it has no problem embracing pictures of God's wrath as a natural part of God's character, equal to God's love. It reads the violence of Scripture as license to exemplify this same kind of action in the world and often quickly moves to an insular understanding of the church's purpose and role in the world. For the hermeneutic of authority, the world is simply the place where God demonstrates God's might, and our job is to bring God glory by distancing ourselves from sin and sinners.

Those holding to a hermeneutic of authority often justify their actions and manipulations as the acts or will of God. Throughout history, many persons who claim to live under the dominion of the God of control have acted in this God's name and claimed his authority but have lacked any of his character. This hermeneutic of authority certainly brings with it the ability to be efficacious in the world, but the uncertainty is whether this efficacy will bring us a kind of world that we want to inhabit or a future that looks anything like the desires of God as seen in Scripture.

On the other hand, a belief in the God of passivity naturally leads to a theology of absence. Since this God is distant, he can only offer us a gospel of autonomy, where we are free to build the future we desire. This vision of God leads us to read Scripture through a *hermeneutic of optimism*.

The hermeneutic of optimism reads Scripture through the lens of human ability and potential. As such, it often reads Scripture as only a moral compass. The absent God is willingly forgotten (this includes the Son and the Holy Spirit), and we come to the Bible to understand right from wrong. Though optimism can certainly be a good thing, a hermeneutic of optimism can lead us to see the tragedies of the world around us and believe that we can make things better on our own. Such a lens often gives us the courage to reimagine our reality in new ways, and even though it may hold the dreams of God at heart, it lacks the efficacy of God in follow-through because it is all done by human power and limited by human imagination. Thus, the world is left hopeless because it is ultimately left godless.

Finally, a theology of luck moves us beyond the categories of control and passivity to reimagining the world through the lens of a God of relationship, who offers us a gospel of participation. As such, we are called to read Scripture through the *hermeneutic of love.*[6]

Reading Scripture through the lens of love is not a naïve way to read Scripture, at least not if we believe that God's very nature is love. At worst, it fails on the side of grace and love. However, at best, it is an attempt to put aside all self-centered, worldly, and unhealthy assumptions, biases, and beliefs and to read the Scriptures anew, guided by the Spirit, thus reflecting the heart of God. In the words of Larry Hurtado, this lens

> forbids us from reducing the interpretative process to an opportunity for the self-expression of the interpreter, and reminds us that interpretation is an opportunity and a responsibility to engage "another" in good faith.[7]

We must, therefore, come to the text with the "other" in mind. A hermeneutic of love necessitates that we read the text to better understand our world and better serve the other. This type of reading requires more of us because it demands that we take the time to listen and understand. We must wrestle with difficult texts and even wrestle with God as we seek to understand how these scriptures reveal God's loving nature. We must also dialogue with those who read the Bible differently from the way we do in order to understand their perspective and discover what we might learn from them. A hermeneutic of love forces us to read in community, both past and present.

This type of reading forces us not only to recognize the complexities of the historic situations that surrounded the authors' writings but also to recognize our own situations. The difference between the two may necessitate a completely dissimilar application that remains true to the underlying conviction of the text. It may also require us to elevate certain aspects of the Bible that appear to be the more dominant and overarching themes, such as love, grace, peace, and human value, as well as the overarching narrative of God's restoration through human participation. At the same time, we must continue to struggle with texts that appear contradictory to these overarching themes. For example, our attitudes toward the complex issues of war, poverty, equality, and homosexuality must first and foremost be governed by the standard of love, which Christ exemplifies.

It is our hope that a hermeneutic of love will move us toward reimagining more fully the loving and relational nature of God and move us more fully toward engaging our world with this same love. It is our hope that our wrestling with Scripture, with God, and with each other will be done in love and for love and that it will bring glory to God.

Now to him who is able to do immeasurably more than all we ask or imagine, according to his power that is at work within us, to him be glory in the church and in Christ Jesus throughout all generations, for ever and ever! Amen. (Eph. 3:20-21)

Questions for Further Reflection or Small Group Discussion

1. What do you think Morgan Freeman's character in *Bruce Almighty* means when he says, "Be the miracle"? Do you agree or disagree with the sentiment?

2. Do you believe perfection is a place God has for us in the future?

3. Do you see yourself as currently participating in God's making everything new? Why or why not?

4. What do you think of Bonhoeffer's assertion that "only in relationship with the other am I free"? How do you think this resonates in our modern culture?

5. React to this quote: "From a kingdom perspective, freedom is not rights but responsibility."

6. Have you ever had a situation in which you questioned your actions because you thought it might be a stumbling block to someone else?

7. What is a hermeneutic of love? How do you think it might reshape the way we live our lives?

For Further Study

Beginner to Intermediate

Brower, Kent. *Holiness in the Gospels*. Kansas City: Beacon Hill Press of Kansas City, 2005.

Greathouse, William M. *Wholeness in Christ: Toward a Biblical Theology of Holiness*. Kansas City: Beacon Hill Press of Kansas City, 1998.

Kirk, J. R. Daniel. *Jesus Have I Loved, but Paul? A Narrative Approach to the Problem of Pauline Christianity*. Grand Rapids: Baker Academic, 2011.

More Advanced

Gorman, Michael J. *Elements of Biblical Exegesis: A Basic Guide for Students and Ministers*. Rev. and exp. ed. Grand Rapids: Baker Academic, 2009.

Jacobs, Alan. *A Theology of Reading: The Hermeneutics of Love*. Boulder, CO: Westview Press, 2001.

Wynkoop, Mildred Bangs. *A Theology of Love: The Dynamic of Wesleyanism*. 2nd ed. Kansas City: Beacon Hill Press of Kansas City, 2015.

NOTES

● ● ●

Introduction

1. James A. Michener, *The Source* (New York: Random House, 1965), 104-20.

2. Ibid., 120; emphasis ours.

3. Stanley Hauerwas and William H. Willimon, *Resident Aliens: Life in the Christian Colony* (Nashville: Abingdon Press, 1989), 95.

Chapter 1

1. The basics of Joshua's story can be found here: Joshua Prager, "Is Our Suffering God's Will?" Cable News Network, http://www.cnn.com/2013/05/22/opinion/prager-our-suffering-Gods-will. For a more detailed account, see his book: Joshua Prager, *Half-Life: Reflections from Jerusalem on a Broken Neck* (San Francisco: Byliner, 2013).

2. Gottfried Wilhelm Leibniz, *Theodicy: Essays on the Goodness of God, the Freedom of Man and the Origin of Evil* (1710; repr., New York: Cosimo, 2009).

3. Ibid., 94.

4. Ibid., 57.

5. An English translation of Voltaire's work can be found here: Voltaire, *Candide*, Literature.org, http://www.literature.org/authors/voltaire/candide/.

6. Ibid., chap. 1, http://www.literature.org/authors/voltaire/candide/chapter-01.html.

7. Michael Gorman, *Inhabiting the Cruciform God: Kenosis, Justification, and Theosis in Paul's Narrative Soteriology* (Grand Rapids: Eerdmans, 2009), 27.

8. Ibid., 30-31.

9. Richard Dawkins, *The God Delusion* (London: Transworld Publishers, 2006), 51.

10. Peter Kirby, "The Antithesis of Marcion," Early Christian Writings, http://www.earlychristianwritings.com/text/antithesis.html (accessed April 20, 2015).

11. A phrase coined by Tertullian (ca. AD 160–ca. AD 225) to explain the Trinity in *Adversus Praxean*. An English translation of this work can be found here: Tertullian, *Against Praxeas*, Early Christian Writings, http://www.early christianwritings.com/text/tertullian17.html (accessed April 22, 2015).

12. E. Frank Tupper, "The Bethlehem Massacre—Christology against Providence?" *Review and Expositor* 88, no. 4 (1991): 415.

13. Ibid., 416.

14. Michael Lodahl, *The Story of God: A Narrative Theology*, 2nd ed. (Kansas City: Beacon Hill Press of Kansas City, 2008), 84.

15. John Wesley, Sermon 116, "What Is Man?" in *The Bicentennial Edition of the Works of John Wesley* (Nashville: Abingdon Press, 1983–), 4:24.

16. Samuel M. Powell, *Discovering Our Christian Faith: An Introduction to Theology* (Kansas City: Beacon Hill Press of Kansas City, 2008), 164-66.

17. Tupper, "Bethlehem Massacre," 415.

Chapter 2

1. Erwin Tulfo, "There Is Indeed a God," *Manila Times*, November 10, 2013, http://manilatimes.net/there-is-indeed-a-god/.

2. Ibid.

3. Ibid.

4. This is likely an understatement, since the Philippines reports being well over 90 percent Christian: "The Philippines—Religion," Philippine Embassy in Belgium, http://philembassy.be/index.php?option=com_content&view=article& id=85&Itemid=195 (accessed April 23, 2015).

5. See also Gregory A. Boyd, *Satan and the Problem of Evil: Constructing a Trinitarian Warfare Theodicy* (Downers Grove, IL: InterVarsity Press, 2001), where he defines *chance*: "An event can be said to have occurred by 'chance' if it has either no *reason* or no *cause* sufficient to explain it" (387).

6. John Sanders, *The God Who Risks: A Theology of Providence* (Downers Grove, IL: InterVarsity Press, 1998), 216.

7. Christopher J. H. Wright, *The God I Don't Understand: Reflections on Tough Questions of Faith* (Grand Rapids: Zondervan, 2008).

8. An example of this view is John M. Frame, "The Problem of Evil," in *Suffering and the Goodness of God*, ed. Christopher W. Morgan and Robert A. Peterson (Wheaton, IL: Crossway Books, 2008), 141-64.

9. Wright, *The God I Don't Understand*, 46.

10. Josephus, *Antiquities*, bk. 13, chap. 5, sec. 9, in *The Works of Josephus: Complete and Unabridged*, ed. and trans. William Whiston (1737; repr., Peabody, MA: Hendrickson, 1987).

11. Don Thorsen, *An Exploration of Christian Theology* (Peabody, MA: Hendrickson Publishers, 2008), 253.

12. *Jewish Encyclopedia*, s.v. "Predestination," http://www.jewishencyclopedia.com/articles/12338-predestination (accessed April 23, 2015).

13. Ibid.

14. William A. Beardslee, "Casting of Lots at Qumran and the Book of Acts," *Novum Testamentum* 4, no. 4 (1960): 245.

15. Ibid., 246.

16. Sanders, in *The God Who Risks*, writes: "The text does not say that God caused or necessitated the events. In fact, the text is remarkably silent regarding any divine activity until Joseph's speeches" (55).

Chapter 3

1. *Slumdog Millionaire*, directed by Danny Boyle and Loveleen Tandan (Fox Searchlight Pictures, Warner Bros., Celador Films, Film4, Pathé Pictures International, 2008), theatrical release.

2. David Leeming, "Fate," in *The Oxford Companion to World Mythology* (Oxford, UK: Oxford University Press, 2005), 132-33; For a more in-depth picture, see "Moirai," Theoi Project, http://www.theoi.com/Daimon/Moirai.html#Birth (accessed April 27, 2015).

3. There are several different views of divine providence; here we speak of the view that is synonymous with hard determinism. See Stanley N. Gundry and Dennis W. Jowers, eds., *Four Views on Divine Providence* (Grand Rapids: Zondervan, 2011), especially the first essay, by Paul Kjoss Helseth, "God Causes All Things," 25-52.

4. Wayne E. Oates, *Luck: A Secular Faith* (Louisville, KY: Westminster John Knox Press, 1995), 5.

5. Ibid.

6. Ibid., 8 and passim.

7. Ibid., 27.

8. Harold Kushner, *When Bad Things Happen to Good People*, 12th ed. (New York: Shocken Books, 2001), 71.

9. Paul Tillich, *Systematic Theology*, vol. 3, *Life and the Spirit, History and the Kingdom of God* (Chicago: University of Chicago Press, 1963), 51.

10. Jürgen Moltmann, *The Crucified God: The Cross of Christ as the Foundation and Criticism of Christian Theology* (London: SCM Press, 1974), 223.

Chapter 4

1. See D. P. O'Mathúna, "Divination, Magic," in *Dictionary of the Old Testament: Pentateuch*, ed. T. D. Alexander and D. W. Baker (Downers Grove, IL: InterVarsity Press, 2003), 193-97.

2. Victor P. Hamilton, *Handbook on the Pentateuch: Genesis, Exodus, Leviticus, Numbers, Deuteronomy* (Grand Rapids: Baker Book House, 1982), 165-66, for 1, 2, 4, 5, 7, 8, 9, 10; Stephen J. Lennox, *God with Us: An Introduction to the Old Testament*, 2nd ed. (Marion, IN: Triangle Publishing, 2009), 91, for 1, 2, 3, 5, 9; and John D. Currid, *Ancient Egypt and the Old Testament* (Grand Rapids: Baker Book House, 1997), 111, for 6.

3. John Day, "Baal (Deity)," in *The Anchor Bible Dictionary*, ed. D. N. Freedman (New York: Doubleday, 1992), 1:547.

4. Patricia J. Berlyn, "Elijah's Battle for the Soul of Israel," *Jewish Bible Quarterly* 40, no. 1 (2012): 57.

5. *The Invention of Lying*, directed by Ricky Gervais and Matthew Robinson (Warner Bros. and Universal Pictures, 2009), theatrical release.

6. Chris Lautsbaugh, "Do Christians Try to Manipulate God?" *NoSuperHeroes.com* (blog), August 23, 2012, http://www.nosuperheroes.com/do-christians-try-to-manipulate-god/.

7. Leslie J. Francis, Emyr Williams, and Mandy Robbins, "The Unconventional Beliefs of Conventional Churchgoers: The Matter of Luck," *Implicit Religion* 9, no. 3 (2006): 311.

8. Ibid., 312.

9. Richard Webster, *The Encyclopedia of Superstitions* (Woodbury, MN: Llewellyn Publications, 2008), 29-30.

10. Michael J. Wilkins, *Matthew*, The NIV Application Commentary (Grand Rapids: Zondervan, 2004), 597.

11. There is much debate over the Greek phrase *pistis Christou* and whether it should be translated "faith in Christ" or "the faith(fulness) of Christ." There is a significant difference in interpretation and application. See Michael F. Bird and Preston M. Sprinkle, eds., *The Faith of Jesus Christ: Exegetical, Biblical, and Theological Studies* (Milton Keynes, UK: Paternoster, 2009).

12. Kent Brower, *Mark*, New Beacon Bible Commentary (Kansas City: Beacon Hill Press of Kansas City, 2012), 252.

Chapter 5

1. Abraham Lincoln, "Meditation on the Divine Will," September 1862, in *Abraham Lincoln, Slavery, and the Civil War: Selected Writings and Speeches*, ed. Michael P. Johnson (New York: Bedford/St. Martin's, 2000), 168.

2. Ronald C. White Jr., "God Willing: Lincoln on the Divine Mystery," *Christian Century* 122, no. 5 (2005): 12.

3. Abraham Lincoln, "Second Inaugural Address," March 4, 1865, in *Abraham Lincoln, Slavery, and the Civil War*, 320-21.

4. Ibid.

5. Ibid.

6. Jim Harries, "Magic, Science and Theology in African Development," *Evangelical Review of Theology* 35, no. 1 (2011): 18.

7. Ibid., 19.

8. The other major translations are a bit better, but not much.

9. Gary M. Burge, *John*, The NIV Application Commentary (Grand Rapids: Zondervan, 2000), 272-73.

10. Ibid., 273.

11. Klyne Snodgrass, *Ephesians*, The NIV Application Commentary (Grand Rapids: Zondervan, 1996), 180.

12. Bruce G. Epperly, "Infinite Freedom, Creativity, and Love: The Adventures of a Non-competitive God," *Encounter* 71, no. 2 (2010): 47.

13. Ibid., 46.

Chapter 6

1. Anthony Horowitz, *The House of Silk: A Sherlock Holmes Novel* (New York: Mulholland Books, 2011).

2. Arthur Conan Doyle, *A Study in Scarlet* (London: BBC Books, 2011), 9.

3. Arthur Conan Doyle, *The Hound of the Baskervilles* (Clayton, DE: Prestwick House, 2006), 116.

4. Michael Reeves, "Three Is the Loveliest Number: Why 'That Trinity Stuff' Is Not a Philosophical Headache but a Captivating Picture of the Good and Beautiful," *Christianity Today* 56, no. 11 (2012): 45.

5. Ronald Heifetz, *Leadership without Easy Answers* (Cambridge, MA: Belknap Press of Harvard University Press, 1994), 49.

6. Ibid., 53.

7. Ibid., 57.

8. Ibid., 58.

9. The following prepositional phrases appear in Paul's writings: *in Christ*, eighty-three times; *in the Lord*, forty-seven times; *in him*, twenty-four times; *into Christ*, eleven times; *into him*, eight times; *with Christ*, four times; *with the Lord*, one time; and *with him*, six times.

10. Albert Schweitzer, *The Mysticism of Paul the Apostle*, trans. William Montgomery (Baltimore: Johns Hopkins University Press, 1998); Constantine R. Campbell, *Paul and Union with Christ: An Exegetical and Theological Study* (Grand Rapids: Zondervan, 2012).

11. Miroslav Volf, *Work in the Spirit: Toward a Theology of Work* (Eugene, OR: Wipf and Stock, 2001), 200.

12. Catherine Keller, "'Be this Fish': A Theology of Creation Out of Chaos," *Word and World* 32, no. 1 (2012): 19.

Chapter 7

1. Natan Ophir, "Soul Mates," in *The Encyclopedia of Love in World Religions*, ed. Y. K. Greenberg, 2 vols. (Santa Barbara, CA: ABC-CLIO, 2008), 2:593.

2. Plato, *Symposium*, trans. Benjamin Jowett, The Internet Classics Archive, http://classics.mit.edu/Plato/symposium.html (accessed April 30, 2015).

3. Ophir, "Soul Mates," 595.

4. Interview with Janet Folger by Laura J. Bagby, "The Right Stuff: Being Your Best While Waiting for God's Best," CBN.com, http://www.cbn.com/family /datingsingles/bagby-janetfolger0304.aspx (accessed April 30, 2015).

5. It was written by Marcus Hummon, Bobby Boyd, and Jeff Hanna in 1994.

6. This is from the Rascal Flatts version, which can be found on their site: http://www.rascalflatts.com/lyrics/discography/feels-like-today#3194-2.

7. Albert Y. Hsu, *Singles at the Crossroads: A Fresh Perspective on Christian Singleness* (Downers Grove, IL: InterVarsity Press, 1997), 78.

8. Jeremy Caplan, "Q & A: Rabbi Harold Kushner," *Time*, October 12, 2006, http://content.time.com/time/arts/article/0,8599,1545682,00.html#ixzz 2nnUYQWHG.

9. Ibid.

10. Shane Claiborne and Jonathan Wilson-Hartgrove, *Becoming the Answer to Our Prayers: Prayer for Ordinary Radicals* (Downers Grove, IL: InterVarsity Press, 2008), 11.

11. Ibid.

12. Rob A. Fringer and Jeff K. Lane, *The Samaritan Project* (Kansas City: House Studio, 2012) 164.

13. Erwin Raphael McManus, *Chasing Daylight: Seize the Power of Every Moment* (Nashville: Thomas Nelson, 2002), 18-19.

Chapter 8

1. Peter Moore, "God Told Me To, Say 38% of Americans," *YouGov*, October 25, 2013, https://today.yougov.com/news/2013/10/25/god-told-me/.

2. Frederick Buechner, *Wishful Thinking: A Seeker's ABC* (San Francisco: HarperCollins, 1993), 118-19.

3. Cornelius Plantinga Jr., *Not the Way It's Supposed to Be: A Breviary of Sin* (Grand Rapids: Eerdmans, 1995), 188.

4. Charity: Water, www.charitywater.org.

5. International Justice Mission, www.ijm.org.

6. Kiva, www.kiva.org.

7. This is Rob's translation from the Greek.

Chapter 9

1. *Bruce Almighty*, directed by Tom Shadyac (Universal Pictures and Buena Vista Pictures, 2003), theatrical release.

2. "*Bruce Almighty*: Quotes," IMDb, http://www.imdb.com/title/tt0315327/quotes.

3. Ibid.

4. Dietrich Bonhoeffer, *Creation and Fall, Temptation: Two Biblical Studies* (New York: Simon and Schuster, 1997), 40.

5. William M. Greathouse, *Wholeness in Christ: Toward a Biblical Theology of Holiness* (Kansas City: Beacon Hill Press of Kansas City, 1998), 29.

6. This is not our own idea. As far as we can ascertain, the first to use this terminology was N. T. Wright, *Christian Origins and the Question of God*, vol. 1, *The New Testament and the People of God* (Minneapolis: Fortress Press, 1992), 64.

7. Larry W. Hurtado, "New Testament Studies at the Turn of the Millennium: Questions for the Discipline," *Scottish Journal of Theology* 52, no. 2 (1999): 175.

A SEARCH FOR AUTHENTIC CHRISTIAN HOLINESS

In this seminal work on holiness, Mildred Bangs Wynkoop brought to the forefront the understanding that holiness is relational. This new edition includes the original text plus a previously unpublished chapter, and several essays from influential voices about Wynkoop's impact.

ISBN: 978-0-8341-3493-5

BEACON HILL PRESS
OF KANSAS CITY

Available online at
BeaconHillBooks.com

Also by Rob A. Fringer & Jeff K. Lane

The Samaritan Project
ISBN: 978-0-8341-2839-2
Also available in ebook formats.

Who is my neighbor?

Fringer and Lane invite you to wrestle with what it means to see, love, and be a neighbor. Whether you read this book alone or in a community, the questions and experiential projects throughout each chapter will provide you with practical ways to serve. Through *The Samaritan Project*, reimagine what it looks like to embody the compassion of a neighbor.